Little Visits for Toddlers

Little Visits Library

Little Visits® for Toddlers

Little Visits® Library Volume 1

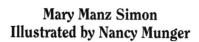

Mary Manz Simon
Illustrated by Nancy Munger

SAINT LOUIS

Scripture quotations marked TEV are from the Good News Bible, the Bible in TODAY'S ENGLISH VERSION. Copyright © American Bible Society 1966, 1971, 1976. Used by permission.

Little Visits® is a registered trademark of Concordia Publishing House.
Little Visits® for Toddlers is an updated version of the previously titled *Little Visits® 1-2-3.*

Copyright © 1990 Concordia Publishing House. Revised copyright © 1995.
3558 S. Jefferson Avenue, St. Louis, MO 63118-3968
Manufactured in the United States of America

1   2   3   4   5   6   7   8   9   10   04   03   02   01   00   99   98   97   96   95

For Hank,
My partner in life

Contents

Preface

The place to begin using this book is on the floor. That is, after all, from where your child views God's world.

The young child's world isn't exotic. It's filled with everyday items such as sandboxes and favorite drinking cups. Places include "my" bedroom, "my" basement, "my" car … with an emphasis on "my." A young child feels the world revolves around him.

You are also a part of that world. You are among those who reflect God's love to a young child. You will be among the first to share the Good News of Jesus Christ as Savior and Lord.

In *Little Visits for Toddlers*, you'll find devotional activities about shadows and storms, naptime and Christmas. Every page includes a special note for you too. You'll find information on child development, snack ideas, and even bits of encouragement. Suggested activities require 30 seconds or less preparation time. I guarantee that! After all, at one time my children were stairsteps aged one, two, and three.

This is the third *Little Visits* book I've written. *Little Visits with Jesus*, a best-seller, was followed by *Little Visits Every Day*. And you now hold the book that comes before the others, the book that will be the first in your child's devotional library.

As an early childhood educator, I can already hear the question, "How soon can I begin using *Little Visits for Toddlers*?" Right now is the perfect time. If your child is six months old or three years old, share devotional time. Use this book informally. Take clues from your child about how long you spend together.

The actual time doing these activities and readings will seem short. But the memories will last a lifetime.

I pray God will bless you, your young child, and your "Little Visits" with Him.

MARY MANZ SIMON

Little Visits® for Toddlers

From the very beginning the Word was with God.

John 1:2

Let's Start

Let's get started; there are many ways.
Let's begin on this first page.
You make the sound or act the part
As we look at ways to start.

Giddyup, giddyup!
The horsy starts.
Giddyup, giddyup!

On your mark, get set, go!
The runners are off.
On your mark, get set, go!

Shake hands, shake hands.
"How do you do?"
Shake hands, shake hands.

"Once upon a time,"
the book begins,
A child grows up with Jesus.
Keep on turning the pages ....

To the adult: *My hope is that this book will become very special for you and your child. Personalize pages as you wish. Perhaps you'll mark in pencil the delightful responses from your child. Perhaps you'll want to jot down the dates on which you use individual devotions. I pray this book will help you and your child make wonderful memories.*

Dear Jesus,
    Help me grow up with You.
    Be with me as I learn and do. Amen.

He gives food to every living creature.

Psalm 136:25

Food Roll

Instructions: Take a can of food and sit on the floor. As you go through the devotion, roll the can between you and your child.

God gives me food.
(*Roll the can.*)

I like good food.
(*Roll the can.*)

Food helps me grow.
(*Roll the can.*)

I'm growing up!
(*Roll the can.*)

To the adult: *Help your child match "real" food with pictures on canned goods. For example, get a carrot out of the refrigerator to match with a carrot pictured on a label.*

Dear Jesus,
    Thank You for food. Amen.

He spreads snow like a blanket.

Psalm 147:16

Snow Fun

Instructions: Act out this verse with your child.

The snowflakes flutter to the
  ground.
I cannot hear a single sound.
I now will run outside to play.
Thank You, God, for snow today!

I wrap a scarf around me tight
And put my mittens on just right.
I run outside for fun and play.
Thank You, God, for snow today!

I roll and roll a great big ball.
Now see my snowman?
  Oh, so tall!
I like this kind of outside play.
Thank You, God, for snow today!

To the adult: *Open your freezer. Ask your child to point to and name things that are as cold as snow.*

Dear Jesus,
 I like to play outside in the snow. Amen.

I urge that ... prayers ... be offered to God.

1 Timothy 2:1

I Pray

Instructions: Act out this verse with your child.

I can pray like this with my
hands together.

I can pray like this when I
kneel at night.

I can pray like this with my
arms across.

I can pray just any way, and
God says, "It's all right."

Dear Jesus,
I pray to You when _____ . Amen.

To the adult: *Help your child explore different respectful positions to use during prayer. Praying with arms folded across the chest— as people did in medieval times—is just one way to pray. This "arms crossed" or pretzel position (as children might say) simply crosses arms, not fingers, as we do when folding our hands to pray. These other postures might be interesting for your child to try.*

See how much the Father has loved us!

1 John 3:1

Emotions

Instructions: Act out this verse with your child.

Sometimes I fuss
And stomp around,
But Jesus still loves me.

Sometimes I'm frightened,
So afraid,
But Jesus still loves me.

Sometimes I'm happy,
Smiling wide,
And Jesus still loves me.

Sometimes I'm angry,
Upset, and mad,
But Jesus still loves me.

What makes me feel so
Glad all over?
Jesus really loves me!

Dear Jesus,
Thank You for loving me. Amen.

To the adult: *Parents spend several years helping their children identify their feelings. A simple verse like this can be a first step toward dealing with emotions in constructive, acceptable ways. During these early stages of emotional development, parents often pray for patience for their child and for themselves.*

Praise the Lord, because He is good.

Psalm 135:3

Happy Birthday!

Instructions: Act out the riddles with your child.

When it's my birthday, I

- blow out the _____ ,
- eat some _____ ,
- open a _____ ,
- listen while people sing

    _____ ,

- and give thanks.

To the adult: *Help your child mark this year's calendar with his birthday. Encourage him to color around the space marking his day, put on a sticker, or show in another way that the day is special.*

Dear Jesus,
   A birthday, a birthday,
   My birthday's just here.
   I don't look much older,
   But thanks, God, for this year. Amen.

*He sets … the time for saving and the time
for throwing away.*　　　　　　　Ecclesiastes 3:6

Clean-Up Time

Instructions: Act out this verse with your child.

> It's clean-up time.
> I'll make the bed.
> Thank You, God, for making
> 　me strong.

> It's clean-up time.
> I'll pick up the toys.
> Thank You, God, for making
> 　me strong.

> It's clean-up time.
> I'll chase the dust.
> Thank You, God, for making
> 　me strong.

> It's clean-up time.
> I'll wash my cup and plate.
> Thank You, God, for making
> 　me strong.

To the adult: *This verse can be repeated throughout the day to
help your child have fun with chores and focus on God.*

Dear Jesus,
Help me be a good helper. Amen.

You created every part of me.

Psalm 139:13

Pairs

Instructions: Act out this verse with your child.

God gave me a pair of hands.
I can clap them.

God gave me a pair of eyes.
I can blink them.

God gave me a pair of thumbs.
I can tap them.

God gave me a pair of feet.
I can touch them.

God gave me a pair of ears.
I can wiggle them.

To the adult: *The concept of pairs might be new to your child. Today, informally help your child identify pairs—shoes, birds' feet, bike tires, etc.*

Dear Jesus,
Thanks for making me, me. Amen.

Worship the Lord your God.

Luke 4:8

Where Are People Going?

Instructions: Act out this verse and make the sounds in it with your child.

People are driving here in cars.
  Zoom, zoom, zoom go the motors.
People are riding here in buses.
  Clink, clink, clink go the coins.
People are walking here on the sidewalk.
  Walk, walk, walk go the feet.
Where are these people going?

People are driving here in cars: zoom, zoom.
People are riding here in buses: clink, clink.
People are walking here on foot: walk, walk.
It's time for church.

Dear Jesus,
  I go to church by _____ .
  Amen.

To the adult: *Young children learn best by doing. Whenever possible, let your child experience different kinds of transportation. Your child might enjoy cutting out pictures of "things I've ridden in" or "things I'd like to ride in" from today's newspaper.*

Let the earth produce all kinds of animal life.

Genesis 1:24

Walking

Instructions: Act out this verse with your child.

God made worms to "walk" like this:
stretch-squoosh, stretch-squoosh.
That's how a worm "walks."

God made penguins to walk like this:
waddle, waddle, waddle, waddle.
That's how a penguin walks.

God made elephants to walk like this:
slowly step, slowly step.
That's how an elephant walks.

God made people to walk like this:
walk, walk, walk, walk.
That's how I walk.

Dear Jesus,
Thanks for my legs. Amen.

To the adult: *Do this verse again, but this time, let your child act it out by letting her "fingers do the walking" in peanut butter play dough. Mix 1 cup peanut butter, ⅔ cup honey, and ½ cup instant nonfat dry milk. (**Tips:** Refrigerate leftover play dough for use tomorrow. Tape waxed paper on the table for easy cleanup.)*

I will always thank the Lord.

Psalm 34:1

Mmmmmm ...

Instructions: Make the sounds described in this verse with your child.

I open my mouth and what do you hear?
Listen to me. Now stand very near.

- I can breathe.

- I can hiss.

- I can hum.

- I can sigh.

- I can cough.

- I can whisper, "Jesus loves me."

To the adult: *Living with a young child often means living with sounds. One of the most effective ways to gain a moment of quiet is to borrow a technique from classroom teachers of young children. Simply whisper, "Listen to the silence."*

Dear Jesus,
    I love You too. Amen.

He spreads snow like a blanket.

Psalm 147:16

Snow Song

Instructions: Sing this to the tune of "Three Blind Mice."

God sends snow.
God sends snow.

Big snow flakes.
Small snow flakes.

Snow falls on houses and down
the trees.
It's carried all over by winter
breeze.
It sticks to my mittens and
makes my nose freeze.

God sends snow.

To the adult: *When children are cooped up inside, water play can brighten even the darkest winter day. The best water toys come from the kitchen: a funnel, turkey baster, and measuring spoons. After play in the sink or tub, your child will appreciate some nice-smelling lotion to keep his skin soft and smooth in the dry winter air.*

Dear Jesus,
   When cold winds blow
   And there is snow,
   I'm glad I'm warm inside. Amen.

I lie down and sleep.

Psalm 3:5

Naptime

I've jumped and run.
I've had some fun.
I've played a bunch.
I've eaten lunch.
It's time to rest.
I'm in my nest.
It's naptime.

To the adult: *One of the nicest aspects of a child going to sleep are the moments spent getting ready for bed. If we think back to our childhood, we might remember a favorite storybook, poem, or prayer. The routine you establish for naptime should settle a child down, establish a quiet mood, and, perhaps years from now, contribute to a happy memory.*

Dear Jesus,
   Thanks for the chance to come to bed
   And on my pillow, rest my head. Amen.

Fruit is sweet to my taste.

Song of Songs 2:3

Snacktime Song

Instructions: Act out this verse with your child as you sing it to the tune of "Here We Go round the Mulberry Bush."

Watch me as I peel a banana,
Peel a banana, peel a banana.
Watch me as I peel a banana.
Thank You, God, for fruit.

Watch me as I open the orange,
Open the orange, open the orange.
Watch me as I open the orange.
Thank You, God, for fruit.

Watch me as I bite the apple,
Bite the apple, bite the apple.
Watch me as I bite the apple.
Thank You, God, for fruit.

To the adult: *Enjoy a fruit break with your child.*

Dear Jesus,
My favorite fruit is _____ .
Amen.

I am with you.

Feelings

Instructions: Act out this verse with your child.

When I feel grumpy,
This is how I frown.

When I'm excited,
I jump up and down.

When I feel loving,
My kisses are free.

When I am frightened,
I need You by me.

To the adult: *A child who is relaxed will talk openly about feelings. A good mid-winter relaxer is playing in the sink with shaving cream. Just squirt some out—your child can trace, draw, or just feel. It's also an easy way to clean the bathroom sink!*

Dear Jesus,
    Thank You for being with me.
    Amen.

*Every kind of animal and bird ... went into the boat
with Noah.* Genesis 7:8–9

Drip Drop

Instructions: Have your child say "drip, drop" at the end
of each line until the end. Then you and your child can
spread your arms to make a rainbow surprise.

> Noah took a hammer.
>> *Drip, drop.*
> He pounded boards together.
>> *Drip, drop.*
> Noah built a big boat.
>> *Drip, drop.*
> The animals all lined up.
>> *Drip, drop.*
> Noah said, "All aboard."
>> *Drip, drop.*
> It rained and rained and rained.
>> *Drip, drop.*
> Noah looked. The rain had
>> stopped. Surprise!

Dear Jesus,
 When it rains, I _____ . Amen.

To the adult: *Your child might enjoy recreating his own version of
Noah's ark. Stuffed animals can be lined up in pairs by a "boat." (A
laundry basket or cardboard box can be the boat.)*

You belong to God, my children.

1 John 4:4

Go-Togethers

Instructions: Help your child make the various shapes using her fingers.

> I can make a ball of snow.
> Snowballs go together with winter.
>
> I can make a heart.
> Hearts go together with Valentine's
> Day.
>
> I can make a tent.
> Tents go together with vacation.
>
> I can make a donut.
> Donuts go together with my
> hungry tummy.
>
> I can make a cross.
> Jesus goes together with me.
>
> Dear Jesus,
> Thank You for my fingers that do
> so many things. Amen.

To the adult: *Syrup shapes can brighten mid-winter breakfasts. Use a cookie cutter to cut out a simple shape in your child's pancake. Then fill the hole with syrup. Or pour the syrup in a familiar shape. Does your child recognize the shape on her pancake?*

God made them all.

Genesis 1:25

And the Sound Is ...

Instructions: Make the sounds described in this verse with your child.

A cow says _____ .
God made cows.

A chicken says _____ .
God made chickens.

A duck says _____ .
God made ducks.

A pig says _____ .
God made pigs.

A turkey says _____ .
God made turkeys.

God made me, too.
But I'm special. I can say,
"Jesus loves me."

To the adult: *Have your child count the number of stuffed toys or plastic animals he has that, if real, might live on a farm.*

Dear Jesus,
I love You too. Amen.

The greatest of these is love.

1 Corinthians 13:13

Hearts

Instructions: Act out this verse with your child.

Snip, snip, cut a heart.
Cut a heart right from the
    start.

Slowly, slowly, move around.
Cut a heart without a sound.

Look, look, what do I see?
It's a heart made just by me!

To the adult: *Valentine's Day is a great holiday for even a young child. If your child can't cut yet, cut out a heart for her. Let her decorate it with glue and bits of red fabric and trim or scraps of red wrapping paper. (Avoid paper doilies—they tear easily.) It will be easier for your child to give away a valentine she's made if she also keeps one of her masterpieces for herself!*

Dear Jesus,
I will give a valentine
to _____ . Amen.

His love is eternal.

Psalm 136:1

Shakes

Instructions: Act out this verse with your child.

What shakes?
- Salt shakes.
- Jelly shakes.
- Earthquakes shake.
- I shake.

God's love doesn't shake.
- It is quiet.
- It tiptoes around.
- It feels like a hug.

To the adult: *The concept of "Jesus as God's valentine" is difficult for young children to understand, but children see that love reflected through people like you. The sharing you do through the activities in this book is one way of demonstrating to a child that "Jesus loves you, and so do I." Happy Valentine's Day to you and the young child in your life.*

Dear Jesus,
Thank You for Your love. Amen.

All night long the Lord protects me.

Psalm 3:5

Shadow Play

Sometimes at night when I get in bed,
I'm ready to rest my tired head.
But I worry about the sounds I hear;
I think up noises that might come
     near.

That's when I lie in bed and take
My fingers, and a cross I make.
The cross reminds me "Jesus is near."
All night long, I know He's here.

Dear Jesus,
     Thank You for watching over me at
     night. Amen.

To the adult: *Shadow play can be more than child's play. Go outside on a bright winter day or set up a bright light to shine against an indoor wall. Show your child how he can make shadow shapes. Your child might even like to take a flashlight and look at all the shadows made by different objects in the house. Seeing how shadows are made—and actually making shadows himself—can reduce a child's fear of shadowy shapes.*

*There will always be cold and heat, summer
and winter, day and night.* Genesis 8:22

When Does It Snow?

Instructions: Act out this verse with your child.

When does it snow?
- Not when the angels have a pillow fight!
- Not when the wind blows white feathers!
- Not when marshmallows fall from the sky!

Snow falls when the air above earth is so cold the water drops freeze.
- Then I put on my snow pants.
- I put on my hat.
- I put on my mittens.
- I put on my boots.
- I go out to play!

Dear Jesus,
Thanks for snow. Amen.

To the adult: *A stick can be a wonderful snow toy. Your child can trace shapes in the snow such as the first letter of her name and even a valentine heart.*

We feast on the abundant food You provide.

Psalm 36:8

Spoons and Fingers

Instructions: Get a knife, fork, and spoon for you and your child to use as you act out this verse. Help your child add words to fill in the blanks.

Spoons are nice
- for ice cream,
- for cereal,
- for _____ .

Forks are good
- for macaroni and cheese,
- for baked potatoes,
- for _____ .

Knives are good
- to spread jelly,
- to cut meat,
- to _____ .

Fingers are good
- for hot dogs,
- for apples,
- for _____ .

To the adult: *Encouraging your child to talk is one of the most important things you can do. Some children find it hard to tell what they are doing. Sometimes it's hard to think and talk at the same time—that's why your child is encouraged to use real utensils for this activity. And while your child learns to talk, you learn to listen. You and your child will use the good verbal and attentive listening skills you are learning right now for many years.*

Dear Jesus,
    Thanks for things to help me eat. Amen.

Love is eternal.

1 Corinthians 13:8

Love Story

Instructions: Each time you read the word *love* in the story, give your child a hug or kiss.

Once upon a time, there was a little child. The child didn't know about Valentine's Day.

"Valentine's Day is a holiday of *love*," said his grandma.

"It's the day of *love*," said his brother.

"It's when people talk of *love*," said his mother.

"But what is *love*?" asked the little boy.

"I *love* you," said his grandma.

"I *love* you," said his brother.

"*Love* is a warm cuddly feeling," said his mother.

"*Love* is what you feel when you talk to Jesus."

To the adult: *What will you do when your child presents you with a genuine child-made valentine? The correct response to any child's artwork is to be honest and positive. For example: "I see you liked red." "Red is such a good color for Valentine's Day." "I can tell you worked so hard on this." "Tell me about this." All responses should be said "in love."*

Dear Jesus,
I love You. Amen.

Pray at all times.

1 Thessalonians 5:17

Nod, Shake, Turn, & Bow

I can nod my head yes.
I can shake my head no.
I can turn it one way
So very slow.

I'll now think inside
What to tell God today.
My head will bow down
Here as I pray.

To the adult: *This verse is an excellent way to settle down a child for prayer. You might want to mark the top of the page for easy reference. This also works well as a "lead-in" to meal-, nap- or nighttime prayers.*

Dear Jesus,
  I like to pray to You. Amen.

He sends the wind.

Psalm 147:18

Blow, Wind, Blow

Instructions: Act out this verse with your child.

God says to the March wind:
   "Blow, wind, blow. Scrape away the
   winter snow. Blow, wind, blow."

God says to the March wind:
   "Softly, move softly. Let the buds burst
   on the trees. Softly, move softly."

God says to the March wind:
   "Be a soft spring breeze. Wave over
   the grass and trees. Be a soft spring
   breeze."

God says to the March wind:
   "Stop, wait, shh! Just whisper over
   river and hill; spring will tiptoe in."

To the adult: *Flying a kite with a young child sounds like a great idea, but often, it's an idea before its time. Few young children successfully fly kites. Instead, try this guaranteed kite. Take an empty plastic bread bag. Dump out the crumbs. Cut three holes near the opening and tie a piece of yarn or string to each hole. Make the strings about 12" long. Then your child can run with it!*

Dear Jesus,
    For winds that blow and winds that sing,
    Thank You, God, for spring. Amen.

Watch for the new thing I am going to do.

Isaiah 43:19

Surprise!

Instructions: Act out this verse with your child.

Surprise!
A jack-in-the-box pops up.

Surprise!
I see baby birds in the nest.
Tweet, tweet.

Surprise!
I blow away the dandelion fluff.

Surprise!
I blow out all the candles on the
birthday cake.

Surprise!
The snowman melts.

To the adult: *The refrigerator door is a great place to store magnets. Some hold up children's artwork. Your child will love playing with magnets on the refrigerator. He'll be close to you in the kitchen, and the "magnet board" is always at the right height. Don't put out all the magnets at one time. Rotate them to build an element of surprise.*

Dear Jesus,
    You don't surprise me. I know
    You're my Jesus. Amen.

When Jesus was twelve years old, they went to the festival as usual.   Luke 2:42

Jesus at Church

Instructions: Ask your child to respond with the words "My Jesus" at the end of each line. This gives her a chance to help "tell" the story of Jesus in the temple.

> Jesus walked to church.
>   *My Jesus.*
> He went with His parents.
>   *My Jesus.*
> Then they couldn't find
>   *my Jesus.*
> Mary asked, "Where is
>   *my Jesus?*"
> Joseph asked, "Where is
>   *my Jesus?*"
> Then Mary saw Him:
>   "*My Jesus!*"
> Then Joseph saw Him:
>   "*My Jesus!*"
> We, too, can say,
>   "*My Jesus.*"

Dear Jesus,
    I'm glad You always know where I am. Amen.

To the adult: *Play hide-and-seek using one of your child's larger toys.*

Lord, You have made so many things!

Psalm 104:24

Squirrels

Instructions: Act out this verse with your child by counting on your fingers.

The furry squirrel peeks out her head,
"God made this day; get out of bed!"
The furry squirrel squeaks in the tree,
"Come out, you little ones, with me."
Now here they come: 1–2–3–4.
They scamper out the tree's front door
And bounce along the tree's big limb.
The first one says, "Can I go in?"
The second says, "It's fun up here."
The third one says, "Oh, do not fear."
The fourth one says, "I see God's world."
And Mother says, "Thank God for squirrels."

Dear Jesus,
My favorite animal is ＿＿＿＿＿ . Amen.

To the adult: *Large-muscle development occurs before small-muscle development. That's one reason fingerplays are such great small-muscle practice for young children. Another basic small-muscle activity is stringing beads. Be sure the beads are large and your child has a well-tipped shoelace to hold them. After stringing several beads, tie a knot. Then if the string falls, your child won't lose all the beads. Even in a simple activity like this, do everything possible for the child to experience success.*

The wind blows wherever it wishes.

John 3:8

Blowin' in the Wind

Instructions: Act out this verse and make the sounds in it with your child.

When a kite flies high, the wind
blows like this _____ .
When storm clouds gather, and
lightening flashes, the wind blows
like this _____ .
When the rain is pouring down, the
wind blows like this

_____ .

When the sun comes out after a
storm, the wind blows like this

_____ .

Today, the wind is blowing like this

_____ .

To the adult: *Children often delight in the wind. Wind blows hair across their faces, and it tickles. Wind flaps clothes and that's fun! Help your child notice wind. Your child can wet the tip of a finger and point it toward the wind. Can your child catch the wind like that?*

Dear Jesus,
    When the wind blows hard, I feel
    _____ . Amen.

Look at my hands.

Luke 24:39

Feely Fingers

Instructions: Help your child move around the room for this verse.

My fingers can feel

- something soft. (*How many things can you touch that are soft?*)

- something hard. (*How many things can you touch that feel hard?*)

- something smooth. (*How many things can you touch that feel smooth?*)

My fingers can feel your fingers! (*Hold hands with your child.*)

To the adult: *Take an empty bag of any kind. Put in, one at a time, objects familiar to your child: a spoon, cup, washcloth. See if your child can name the object just by feeling. (No peeking!)*

Dear Jesus,
    Thank You for my feely fingers. Amen.

I have cared for you from the time you were born.
                                              Isaiah 46:3

Baby Days

Instructions: Act out this verse with your child.

When I was a baby,

- I slept.

- I cried.

- I learned to roll over.

- I learned to sit up.

- I learned to crawl.

- I learned to stand up.

Now I can say …

To the adult: *We often focus on the growth of our young child. But the little one isn't the only one who grows. Think back: How have you grown as a caregiver in the past months? God has blessed your growing, too.*

Dear Jesus,
  Thank You for helping me grow up.
  Amen.

All living things look hopefully to You.

Psalm 145:15

Woof! Woof!

Instructions: Act out this verse with your child.

Dogs like to dig.
They use their paws.
God gave dogs digging paws.

Dogs like to sniff.
They bury their bones.
God gave dogs sniffy noses.

Dogs like to wag.
They wag their tails.
God gave dogs waggy tails.

Dogs like to bark.
They say, "Woof, woof."
God gave dogs woofy voices.

I like to pray.
I talk to God and say,
"Thank You, God, for dogs. Amen."

Dear Jesus,
   Thank You for dogs. Amen.

To the adult: *Dogs can be big, noisy, and overly friendly. Those same qualities that appeal to older children may make younger children afraid. Gently introduce your child to dogs—perhaps using a stuffed animal or by visiting a pet shop.*

He is not here—He has been raised!

Mark 16:6

Happy Easter

Instructions: Act out this verse with your child.

A little springtime bunny goes
hop, hop, hop.

A little springtime chick says,
"Peep, peep, peep."

A little child of God goes
clap, clap, clap.

He's risen! He's risen!
Jesus is alive.

Clap, clap, clap.

Dear Jesus,
Thank You for being my Savior.
Amen.

To the adult: *Look around the house with your child for signs of Easter.*

Through Him God created everything in heaven and on earth. Colossians 1:16

Balancing Acts

Instructions: Give your child a washcloth to act out this verse.

I can balance a washcloth on my
   shoulder.
God gave me a great shoulder.

I can balance a washcloth on my
   head.
God gave me a great head.

I can balance a washcloth on my
   hand.
God gave me a great hand.

I can balance a washcloth on my
   foot.
God gave me a great foot.

I can balance a washcloth on my
   tummy.
Whoops! I'm going to laugh!

To the adult: *Make a beanbag for your child. Sew two washcloths together and use dry beans for stuffing. On a dry day outdoors, your child can hide the beanbag, play catch with you, or do balancing acts.*

Dear Jesus,
    Thanks for all my parts. Amen.

You soften the soil with showers and cause
the young plants to grow. Psalm 65:10

Here Comes Spring

Instructions: Stand outside or look out a window as you and your child read this verse.

I see a sign of spring.
It flies. It hunts for worms.
It says, "Tweet, tweet."
It is a _____ .

I hear a sign of spring.
It goes drip, drop.
It makes splashy puddles.
It is _____ .

I feel a sign of spring.
It makes the trees blow.
It keeps kites up in the sky.
It is _____

I see a sign of spring.
It is green.
It pushes out of the ground.
It is _____ .

To the adult: *Children and adults are usually so glad to get out of the house in spring that it's easy to miss some of the beauty. This spring, take time to help your child observe the buds on a tree branch, a drop of rain plunking in a puddle, the first dandelion in the lawn. Looking closely at the miracles of spring helps us focus on the majesty of God, our Creator.*

Dear Jesus,
 Thank You for spring. Amen.

He has been raised.

Luke 24:6

1, 2, 3

Instructions: Help your child use her fingers for this verse. There are some tricky spots, so ask your child to listen carefully.

> 1, 2, 3
>> Jesus rose for me.
>
> 3, 4, 5
>> Jesus is alive.
>
> 5, 6, 7
>> Jesus reigns in heaven.
>
> 8, 9, 10
>> It's Easter time again.
>
> Hallelujah!

To the adult: *This type of rhyme is more difficult than simple finger counting. Older children will delight in the challenge. Help younger ones with the activity so they feel good about their actions, too.*

Dear Jesus,
   I'm glad You rose on Easter. Amen.

Learn what I teach you.

Proverbs 2:1

Do This, Do That

Instructions: Act out this verse with your child.

Put your two hands on your head;
Then reach way up high.

Put your hands down at your sides;
And stretch up to the sky.

Put your feet all tight together;
Now jump 1–2–3.

We'll end with hands together
So you can pray with me.

To the adult: *This "Simon says" technique also works well when your child needs to get dressed or pick up the toys. Make chores into a game, and they'll get done faster.*

Dear Jesus,
  Thank You for this time together. Amen.

God is our shelter and strength.

Psalm 46:1

Moving

Instructions: Act out this verse with your child.

People move to a new house.
They pack boxes. Pack, pack, pack.
And God goes with them.

People move to a new house.
They load boxes into a van.
   Load, load, load.
And God goes with them.

People move to a new house.
They drive the moving van.
   Drive, drive, drive.
And God goes with them.

People move to a new house.
They unpack the boxes.
   Unpack, unpack, unpack.
And God goes with them.

People move to a new house.
They shake hands with new friends.
   Shake, shake, smile!
And God goes with them.

To the adult: *Moving to a new place can be a bother to an adult. Moving to a new place can mean excitement and fun or outright fear for a child. A child who moves gets tremendous comfort from familiar routines such as daily devotions and prayers. During a move, keep basic living patterns as normal as possible, and always give thanks to God for His help.*

Dear Jesus,
   I'm glad You're always with me. Amen.

You created every part of me.

Psalm 139:13

All around a Chair

Instructions: Pull a chair into the middle of the room and act out this verse with your child.

> I can crawl under the chair.
> Look at me go under.
> God gave me a great body.
>
> I can walk around the chair.
> Look at me go around.
> God gave me a great body.
>
> I can walk backwards around the chair.
> Look at me go around backwards.
> God gave me a great body.
>
> I can sit on the chair.
> Look at me on top.
> Now hear me pray.
>
> Dear Jesus,
> Thank You for all the ways I can move.
> Amen.

To the adult: *Early childhood educators identify learning spatial relationships as a goal young children should achieve. One aspect of that concept is understanding what some prepositions really mean. "Around," "under," and "on top of" are things a child learns through daily activities. Give your child every opportunity to have fun experimenting with these words, using the great body God has given.*

Be glad ... because of your Creator.

Sounds of Spring

Instructions: Act out this verse with your child.

A lawn mower mows.
A bee goes buzz.
(*Clap!*)
God gave me spring.

A bird goes tweet.
A hose squirts water.
(*Clap!*)
God gave me spring.

The warm wind whispers.
The raindrops plunk.
(*Clap!*)
God gave me spring.

Dear Jesus,
   I hear spring when _____ .
   Amen.

To the adult: *Spring brings so many delights to children that they often miss the sounds. Stop for a moment. Listen to spring. What sounds can your child identify?*

Praise Him with drums.

Psalm 150:4

A Jesus Drum

Instructions: Give your child an empty coffee can, oatmeal container, or kitchen pot. Help your child use his drum.

Rum-dee-dum.
Rum-dee-dum.
I can play my Jesus drum.

Rum-dee-dum.
Rum-dee-dum.
I march with my Jesus drum.

Rum-dee-dum.
Rum-dee-dum.
Listen to my Jesus drum.

To the adult: *Your child can decorate a "Jesus drum" that can be used again. Ask your child to color on a piece of paper. Tape it around the pot or container used for this activity. Next time you feel a need to change the mood, bring out the Jesus drum.*

Dear Jesus,
   I like to talk to You. Amen.

Remember your Creator while you are still young.
Ecclesiastes 12:1

Swing into Spring

Instructions: Act out this verse with your child.

My arms can swing.
My voice can sing,
"Thank You, God, for spring."

My arms can swing.
My legs can swing.
My voice can sing,
"Thank You, God, for spring."

My arms can swing.
My legs can swing.
My body swings.
My voice can sing,
"Thank You, God, for spring."

To the adult: *Poets say God's earth wakes up in spring. Twelve months makes a big difference to a child. Last spring, your child couldn't—developmentally—enjoy spring as she does this year. Enjoy the outdoors with your young child.*

Dear Jesus,
    Thank You for spring. Amen.

*Everything that happens in this world happens
at the time God chooses.*　　　　　Ecclesiastes 3:1

The Spring Robin

Instructions: Sing this to the tune of "The Farmer in the Dell."

The robin found a worm.
The robin found a worm.
Hooray! God gives us spring.
The robin found a worm.

The robin builds a nest.
The robin builds a nest.
Hooray! God gives us spring.
The robin builds a nest.

The baby birdies tweet.
The baby birdies tweet.
Hooray! God gives us spring.
The baby birdies tweet.

To the adult: *Help your child make up his own stanzas to this song.*

Dear Jesus,
I like to sing.
Thank You for spring. Amen.

He will … guide our steps into the path of peace.
Luke 1:78–79

Neat Feet

Instructions: Have your child go barefoot for this activity.

God gave me feet
So I can walk around.
God gave me feet
As I tiptoe, not a sound.
God gave me feet
That I can wiggle, wiggle, wiggle.
God gave me feet
That someone can tickle!

Dear Jesus,
Thanks for my neat feet. Amen.

To the adult: *While your child is barefoot, trace around her feet. Have her stand with heels touching. Add a few antennae, and she'll have her own butterfly feet to color.*

God loves the one who gives gladly.

2 Corinthians 9:7

Money, Money

Instructions: Drop loose change into a little bag. Your child can shake it every time you say the words, "Money, money."

Coins make noise. *Money, money.*
Coins are heavy. *Money, money.*
Coins pay the doctor. *Money, money.*
Coins help children *Money, money.*
Learn about Jesus. *Money, money.*
Let's take coins *Money, money.*
To church on Sunday. *Money, money.*

Dear Jesus,
 Thanks for money to give at church.
 Amen.

To the adult: *After your child is beyond the risk of swallowing coins, give your child many opportunities to touch coins. They can be sorted by color and kind. Also give your child the chance to learn how to make change. A fun way of doing this is to put price tags (1¢, 5¢, 10¢) on food cans in the pantry. Then play store. If you do this after shopping, your child can even help put the groceries away!*

When I was a child, my speech, feelings, and thinking were all those of a child. 1 Corinthians 13:11

Babytimes

Instructions: Act out this verse with your child.

When I was just a little babe, I lived inside my bed.
I slept and slept and slept and slept; I could not lift my head.
But soon I looked around to see this world that God has made.
I saw some people, colors, movements, dark and light and shade.
I learned to roll from front to back and then the other way.
It seemed I learned, at least, a single brand-new thing each day.
But that was, oh, so long ago, and now I'm all grown up;
I feed myself, know how to eat, and drink right from a cup.
And even though I'm now so big, each day I spend some time
To thank my family and my Lord, who helped me grow up fine.

To the adult: *Putting items in order by size is an early learning skill. Your child can do this easily by lining up items beginning with the smallest and ending with the largest. Outdoors, your child can make a line of sticks, stones, or anything that is safe for play and will show progression of size. Very young children might say, "This is the baby stick, the sister stick, and the mommy stick" or use similar words to understand the concept of big, bigger, biggest.*

Dear Jesus,
Thank You for helping me grow. Amen.

The Lord is risen indeed!

Luke 24:34

An Easter Child

Instructions: Act out this verse with your child.

I'm an Easter child.
I can clap my hands.
Jesus is alive.

I'm an Easter child.
I can lift my shoulders.
Jesus is alive.

I'm an Easter child.
I can blink my eyes.
Jesus is alive.

I'm an Easter child.
I can nod my head.
Jesus is alive.

To the adult: *The concept of Easter is almost impossible for a young child to understand. Very young children can simply be told that, on Easter, we celebrate that "Jesus is alive."*

Dear Jesus,
    Thank You for making Easter. Amen.

Teach a child how he should live.

Proverbs 22:6

Church Time

Instructions: Act out this verse with your child.

I like to go to church
Where I can sing and pray.
But I won't roller-skate to church;
At least I won't today!

I like to go to church
Where I can sing and pray.
But I won't ride a bike to church;
At least I won't today!

I like to go to church
Where I can sing and pray.
But I won't fly a kite to church;
At least I won't today.

I like to go to church
Where I can sing and pray.
But I won't jump a rope to church;
At least I won't today!

To the adult: *Too often, parents of young children go to church hoping to "survive" another Sunday. To ensure your own personal joyful worship, start Sunday morning on Saturday night by setting out the breakfast dishes and laying out church clothes for you and your child. Make plans to keep your child occupied while you dress. Consider using a short video from a Christian bookstore or* Little Visits on the Go *with audiocassette or* My Bible Stories *with audiocassette.*

Dear Jesus,
    I'm glad I can go to church. Amen.

Praise Him ... all animals, tame and wild,
reptiles and birds. Psalm 148:9–10

Blanket Butterfly

Instructions: You'll need a bath towel or blanket for this verse. Act out the life cycle of the butterfly with your child.

God makes a butterfly happen in a special
way.
He has it live as a caterpillar for many, many
days.
It squiggles forward, squiggles back, like a
big fat worm.
It wiggles all around and makes a flip-flop
kind of turn.
(*Wiggle under blanket.*)

When God says, "The time is up," it spins a
nice cocoon
Where it's all quiet, dark, and cozy, like a
little room.
(*Stay quiet under blanket.*)

But God knows best and is in charge of every
living thing.
So one day the skin goes "crack;" a butterfly
sees spring.
(*Pop up from blanket.*)

To the adult: *Your child can make a "caterpillar salad." Have him arrange grapes or melon balls in a squiggly line on a lettuce leaf.*

Dear Jesus,
    Thanks for pretty butterflies. Amen.

Come, let us bow down and worship Him.

Psalm 95:6

I Can Count

Instructions: Help your child count along with the verse.

God gave me knees;
I'll count up to two.
God gave me eyes
Just to see you.

God gave me fingers;
I'll count up to ten.
God gave me toes.
I'll count ten again!

I've only one nose;
That's where I smell.
With all of these parts,
See? God made me well.

To the adult: *Help your child focus on different parts of the body by using easy-to-make binoculars. Tape together two empty toilet paper rolls. What can your child see?*

Dear Jesus,
   Thanks for hands to fold when
   I pray. Amen.

*As long as the world exists, there will be a
time for planting.*　　　　　　　　Genesis 8:22

Happy Spring!

Instructions: Ask your child to echo the words you say.
Begin very, very softly; end with a loud, "Happy spring!"

Springtime is	*Springtime is*
Coming soon.	*Coming soon.*
Look for flowers	*Look for flowers*
That will bloom.	*That will bloom.*
God made spring	*God made spring*
With skies so blue.	*With skies so blue.*
God made spring	*God made spring*
For me and you.	*For me and you.*
Happy spring!	*Happy Spring!*

Dear Jesus,
　　Thank You for the springtime. Amen.

To the adult: *Tossing confetti is one of the easiest ways to express a
spirit of celebration. Ask your child to color paper, using spring colors. Then she can cut pieces, any shape or size. (If your child is just
learning to cut, hold a piece of paper while she goes "open close,
open close" with the scissors.) Using your child's own version of
confetti, read this echo verse again. You and your child can toss
the confetti when you say, "Happy spring!" Your child probably will
eagerly clean up the confetti—just to do the verse with you again!*

The Lord created the earth.

Crawl Around

Instructions: Act out this verse with your child.

I can crawl like a snake, slither on
the ground.
I can crawl like a worm, on the side-
walk, all around.
I can crawl like a caterpillar who'll
soon fly away.
I can crawl like a baby, for I used to
move that way.
All these crawling, creeping creatures
were made by God above.
He created them and keeps them in
His holy love.

Dear Jesus,
Thanks for making me. Amen.

To the adult: *Crawling is one of the most common actions we observe in the play of young children. When you watch your child at play during the next few weeks, notice how often he naturally moves on his stomach.*

The earth is filled with Your creatures.

Psalm 104:24

Wake Up!

Instructions: Act out this verse with your child.

What wakes up in spring?
Bears wake up.
  They stretch and stretch.
Snakes wake up.
  They slither around.
Bees wake up.
  They buzz, buzz.
Beavers wake up.
  They slap, slap.

A beautiful spring day dawns.
  The sun shines.
The breeze blows gently.

The owl says, "Hoot, hoot,"
  and goes back to sleep.

To the adult: *Help your child uncover some of the animals of spring. Turn over a leaf, a rock, a log. Prepare your child in advance—a young child might be frightened, or delighted, to see all the scurrying once the cover is removed from an animal's hiding place.*

Dear Jesus,
    Thanks for the signs of spring. Amen.

You send abundant rain on the plowed fields.

Psalm 65:10

Pitter Pat

Instructions: Have your child tap her fingers on a table and say, "Pitter pat," as indicated.

Rain drops.
Pitter pat.

Water flowers.
Pitter pat.

Wash the cars.
Pitter pat.

Bathe the birds.
Pitter pat.

Clean the streets.
Pitter pat.

Make some puddles.
Pitter pat.

Splash, splash, splash.
Pitter pat.

To the adult: *After a spring rain, while the sidewalks are still wet, give your child some colored chalk. Your child's drawings will be vivid in color and wash off easily with the next rain.*

Dear Jesus,
    Thanks for rain. Amen.

In the countryside the flowers are in bloom.

Song of Songs 2:12

Flowers

Instructions: Act out this verse with your child.

Before there is a flower,
   there is a tiny seed.
I dig a hole and drop it in.
Where is my flower now?

Before there is a flower,
   God makes the raindrops fall.
I watch the drops go pitter pat.
Where is my flower now?

Before there is a flower,
   God makes the sun shine
      bright.
I watch the shadows play.
Where is my flower now?

Look! Now I see a flower.
   God sends the sun and rain.
My flower is so pretty.
I'll go back and plant again.

To the adult: *This is an easy story for your child to act out for friends or relatives. Informally sharing this kind of "story" can help a child build a positive self-image.*

Dear Jesus,
Thanks for Your pretty flowers. Amen.

The winter is over.

Song of Songs 2:11

An In-Out Day

Instructions: Give your child a small towel for this activity. Whenever a line begins with *Whoops!*, he can hide underneath the towel.

The day is started; I'll go out to play.
Whoops! There's a cloud. It's an in-out day.

The cloud has flown. It's far away.
Whoops! There's another. It's an in-out day.

The sun is bright; now I can play.
Whoops! Time to eat! It's an in-out day.

Back and forth, I know it's May.
Whoops! It's the month for in-out days.

Dear Jesus,
   Wherever I am, I know You're with me.
   Amen.

To the adult: *Now—before the hot weather—is the best time to be sure your child will have a shady outdoor play area. Children's internal thermometers don't regulate as well as adults'. They can get overheated without being aware of it. Putting the sandbox in the shade, or having a corner to dig under a tree, can make a safer, happier summer.*

You provide food, and they are satisfied.

Psalm 104:28

Finger Foods

Instructions: Ask your child to show the shape of each food mentioned.

Of all the foods God gives me,
The ones I like the most
Are apples, crunchy carrot sticks,
And in the morning, toast.

You see these foods are special;
I eat them by myself.
So I thank God for finger foods
That are good for my health.

Dear Jesus,
   I like to eat _____ .
   Amen.

To the adult: *One standard finger food for young children is a sandwich. The next time you serve one to your child, use a cookie cutter to cut out the bread, meat, and cheese. A shapely sandwich will be lots of fun to eat!*

The air is fragrant with blossoming vines.

Song of Songs 2:13

Buzz, Buzz

Instructions: Help your child count on her fingers the number of bees mentioned.

The first little bee flew out of the hive.

The second one buzzed, "Thank God I'm alive."

The third little bee buzzed off to some clover.

The fourth little bee said, "Please move over."

The fifth little bee looked round to say, "Thank You, God, for this beautiful day."

To the adult: *Some young children have difficulty learning the ordinals or numerical positions. There is nothing to suggest that learning the concepts "first, second, third" is really difficult. Often, we just don't make a point of labeling items in this way. Next time you are counting silverware, or lining up shoes, say, "This is the first, second …" This is an easy way to help your child expand her basic understanding of 1, 2, 3.*

Dear Jesus,
    On this early summer day,
    Thanks for this weather is what
    I say. Amen.

He breathed life-giving breath into ... the man.

Genesis 2:7

I Can Blow It!

Instructions: Act out this verse with your child.

I can blow it!
Watch me blow a dandelion.

I can blow it!
Watch me blow a pinwheel.

I can blow it!
Watch me blow a trumpet.

I can blow it!
Watch me blow bubbles.

To the adult: *Look through a magazine with your child. Help him find pictures of things that move with the wind.*

Dear Jesus,
    For air that I can blow
    And eyes that see things go,
    Thank You, Jesus. Amen.

[God's] love is so great that we are called God's children.   1 John 3:1

Sayings

Instructions: Ask your child to answer the questions.

Who says:

- Oink, oink?

- Let's eat?

- Tweet, tweet?

- I love you?

Jesus loves you too!

To the adult: *A young child experiences the love of Christ through people like you. The way you care, forgive, and share is one way Jesus' love touches the young. Our Lord is working through you to touch the life of the child with whom you share this book. Thanks be to Him!*

Dear Jesus,
    I love You. Amen.

Come, let us praise the Lord!

Psalm 95:1

Going to Church

Instructions: Act out this verse with your child.

> When I go to church, I sing,
>   sing, sing.
> God gave me a voice to praise
>   Him.
>
> When I go to church, I smile,
>   smile, smile.
> God gave me a mouth to show
>   joy.
>
> When I go to church, I hold
>   another hand.
> God gave me hands to bring
>   others.
>
> When I go to church, I pray,
>   pray, pray.
> God is always near to listen.

To the adult: *Does your child have a friend who could be invited to church? Offer to take the child with you. Your young one might be on best behavior by bringing a friend, and you'll be planting the concept of being Jesus' helper.*

Dear Jesus,
    Thank You for my church. Amen.

Let the earth produce all kinds of animal life.

Genesis 1:24

Animals, Animals

Instructions: Act out this verse with your child.

A bear in the forest might sleep in a cave. That's no pet for me.

A lion in the grasslands might roar aloud. That's no pet for me.

A monkey in the jungle might climb a tree. That's no pet for me.

God made cats and dogs so soft and warm to hug.

Now those are pets for me.

To the adult: *With your child, look for a picture of an animal in the newspaper. Discuss whether or not it would make a good pet.*

Dear Jesus,
    I like some animals like _____ .
Amen.

Be glad, fields, and everything in you!

Psalm 96:12

Yum, Yum

Instructions: Select several fruits or vegetables, each of a different color. Set the food on the table in front of your child and play this color game.

God gives us food to eat that's green.
What do you see that's green?

God gives us food to eat that's yellow.
What do you see that's yellow?

God gives us food to eat that's red.
What do you see that's red?

God gives us food that you like to eat.
What is your favorite food?

Dear Jesus,
Thank You for good things to eat.
Amen.

To the adult: *Encourage your child to group the foods on the table in different ways: things that grow under the ground or foods that animals like too. Do this only if your child seems to enjoy (and be ready for) this activity.*

Be happy while you are still young.

Ecclesiastes 11:9

Legwork

Instructions: Ask your child to lie on her back on the carpet.

Let's pretend: kick your legs in
the air like you are

- swimming,

- jumping,

- walking.

Now let's do everything again,
right side up!

Dear Jesus,
I'm learning to move in so many ways.
Thank You, Jesus, for these great days.
Amen.

To the adult: *Informally introduce your child to hopping on one foot and jumping with two feet. Wait, though, with skipping. Skipping is a complicated activity that some children—especially boys—don't learn until the age of six, seven, or even later.*

Let the children come to Me.

Luke 18:16

Puppet Talk

Instructions: Make a paper-bag puppet. Draw a simple face on the bottom of an empty brown bag. Let the puppet tell this story. Fill in the blanks with names that mean the most to your child.

Hi! My name is Baggy. I came to your house, right here on _____
Street, to tell you about Jesus.
You know about Jesus. He knows about you,
_____ . Jesus is your Savior.
One of the places you learn about Jesus is at
_____ Church. I know one of your
favorite people there is _____ .
You can learn about Jesus right here too.
Do you know where the Bible is kept?
Ask someone to read to you about when
little children came to see Jesus.
Bye-bye for now. Can you wave to me?

To the adult: *Let your child have some puppet fun too. A mismatched sock makes a good puppet for a young child. Draw a face on the sock with a marking pen. Your child's puppet can talk to Baggy.*

Dear Jesus,
     Thank You for the Bible. Amen.

Be glad, earth and sky!

Psalm 96:11

I See and Hear

Instructions: Act out this verse and make the sounds in it with your child.

In summer, I hear a dog bark.
  I see a tail wag.

In summer, I hear a church bell
  ring. I see people walking.

In summer, I hear a mower start.
  I see the grass get cut.

In summer, I hear a siren whine.
  I see people getting help.

In summer, I hear,
  "Let's go swimming."
  I run for my swimsuit!

To the adult: *You and your child can try listening for this summer sound. Put your ear to the grass. Get as close as possible. Now someone else can walk up to the person on the ground. Can you hear the footsteps?*

Dear Jesus,
   Thanks for my ears that hear and
my eyes that see. Amen.

Listen to the noise.

Isaiah 13:4

Animal Talk

Instructions: Act out this verse with your child.

Buzz, buzz, buzz.
God made a bee.
I buzz too.
Listen to me.

Meow, meow, meow.
God made a cat.
I meow too.
Listen to that.

Talk, talk, talk.
God made me.
I can talk.
Thanks, God, for me.

To the adult: *What other animal sounds can your child identify? Make one sound at a time to see if your child can name which animal moos, quacks, neighs, and hee-haws.*

Dear Jesus,
    I can make all different kinds of noises.
    Amen.

He fills my life with good things.

Psalm 103:5

See 'n' Tell

Instructions: Play this word game with your child.

> I'm looking for something we
>   sit on. What do I see?
> I'm looking for something that
>   turns on. What do I see?
> I'm looking for someone Jesus
>   forgives. Whom do I see?
> I'm looking for something we
>   walk on. What do I see?
> I'm looking for someone Jesus
>   loves. Whom do I see?
> I'm looking for something that
>   gets hot. What do I see?
> I'm looking for someone who
>   loves Jesus. Whom do I see?
>
> Dear Jesus,
>   Thank You
>   for _____ . Amen.

To the adult: *Use this game in the car. Play it with different categories of items: things God gives to help us move around, animals God made, etc.*

He has set the right time for everything.

Ecclesiastes 3:11

Tick Tock

Instructions: You and your child can pretend to be a clock pendulum. Stand straight, with hands at your sides. Step on one foot and then the other, back and forth, to act out the pendulum movement.

> Time to get up.
> Time for today.
> Time now to eat.
> Time now to play.
> Time to go out.
> Time to go here.
> Time to go in.
> Time to go there.
> Time to slow down.
> The end of a day.
> Time to pray.

> Dear Jesus,
> Thank You for this summer day.
> For all I did, thank You, I pray. Amen.

To the adult: *The pattern of a typical day can give a child a sense of security. This is especially important when seasons—and perhaps schedules too—change. But some things stay the same: getting dressed, mealtimes, and Jesus time.*

The angels in heaven … are always in the presence of My Father. Matthew 18:10

Summer Sleep-Overs

Instructions: Ask your child to say, "Jesus sends His angels," at the end of each verse.

We might sleep in a cabin
On a summer trip.
But we aren't all alone:
Jesus sends His angels.

We might sleep in a tent
On a summer trip.
But we aren't all alone:
Jesus sends His angels.

We might sleep in a hotel
On a summer trip.
But we aren't all alone:
Jesus sends His angels.

We might sleep in
a _____
On a summer trip.
But we aren't all alone:
Jesus sends His angels.

To the adult: *The concept of a guardian angel is certainly comforting to a parent. Children, too, can feel God's presence through His "messenger," which is what angel means. Talk about today's Scripture reading with your young child. Your child will probably draw a mental picture of his angel.*

Dear Jesus,
 Thank You for sending me an angel. Amen.

You show Your care for the land.

Psalm 65:9

Four Seasons

Instructions: Act out this verse with your child.

There are four seasons of the year:
Fall, winter, spring, and summer.
I can count them on my fingers,
And they are four in number.

In fall the temperature gets cool.
I put on warmer clothes,
For winter will be coming soon,
As everybody knows.

The earth sleeps soundly, then wakes up.
Birds build their nests and sing:
"Peep, peep, peep, peep, peep,
    peep, peep, peep.
Cheer up! It's time for spring."

Now summer time is finally here.
We can look back and say:
"God made the seasons.
    Thank You, Lord,
Today and every day."

To the adult: *Learning about seasons is an abstract concept for young children. They will learn most easily about yearly changes when you talk and do different things in the different seasons. For example, children might associate spring with "my birthday," summer with swimming, and winter with Jesus' birthday.*

Dear Jesus,
    Thank You for summer. Amen.

Your greatness is seen in all the world!

Let's Hike

Instructions: Act out this verse with your child.

I'm going on a hike.
I might see something that blooms.
That might be a _____ ,
   and God made it.

I'm going on a hike.
I might see something with four legs.
That might be a _____ ,
   and God made it.

I'm going on a hike.
I might see something with pretty wings.
That might be a _____ ,
   and God made it.

To the adult: *A walk down the street can be turned into a kid-size hike. Take a plastic container of juice and trail mix (round cereal, raisins, and mini-marshmallows) in a plastic bag. Add a bathroom towel (for sitting under a tree) and a compass or flashlight, if desired.*

Dear Jesus,
   Thank You for this pretty world. Amen.

A gentle answer quiets anger.

Proverbs 15:1

I Can Hear You!

Instructions: Ask your child to repeat your words.

(Say loudly:)
I love you.
 I love you.
Jesus loves you.
 Jesus loves you.

(Say in a normal tone of voice:)
I love you.
 I love you.
Jesus loves you.
 Jesus loves you.

(Whisper:)
I love you.
 I love you.
Jesus loves you.
 Jesus loves you.

(Whisper the prayer:)

To the adult: *The next time you feel like yelling at your child, try a whisper instead. Soft voices—which force children to pay attention—can be more effective than loud voices. Really!*

Dear Jesus,
    Thank You for loving me. Amen.

The hillsides are full of joy.

Psalm 65:12

What Do Flowers Say?

Instructions: Make two facial-tissue "talking flowers." Crumple a tissue into a tight ball and cover it with another. Loosely wrap a rubber band around the "neck" of the flower. Make it loose enough to wear over your finger. Draw a simple face. Place one flower on your child's finger, another on yours.

> (*Your flower says:*)
> The sun shines so bright. I want
>   to smile.
> (*Child's flower says:*)
> Thank You, God, for summer.
> (*Your flower says:*)
> The rain is so wet. I want to
>   smile.
> (*Child's flower says:*)
> Thank You, God, for summer.
> (*Your flower says:*)
> The breeze is so warm. I want to
>   smile.
> (*Child's flower says:*)
> Thank You, God, for summer.

To the adult: *Your child might want to continue using the puppets after this devotion. Listen carefully to what the puppets "say." Children sometimes talk in a "secondhand" way. They might talk through puppets about things they might not discuss as themselves.*

Dear Jesus,
    Thank You for summer. Amen.

Play drums ... in praise of Him.

Psalm 149:3

A Jesus Parade

Instructions: Give your child a pot and spoon for this activity. March around the room with your child as you read the verse.

March 2–3–4
March 2–3–4
I love Jesus.
I love Jesus.
March 2–3–4
March 2–3–4
Jesus loves me.
Jesus loves me.

Dear Jesus,
I love You. Amen.

To the adult: *Your child can enjoy banging an upside-down pan with a spoon. This is a great activity while you are in the kitchen preparing a meal. A large plastic spoon and a plastic ice-cream bucket make less noise than metal spoons and pans.*

Come, let us praise the Lord!

Psalm 95:1

Let's Go to Church

Instructions: This is an adaptation of the popular children's clapping game "We're going on a bear hunt." Slap your thighs at each italicized word. For more fun, sit cross-legged on the floor facing your child.

> We're *going for* a *car* ride.
> Get *in* the *car* now.
>> Let's *go* to *church.*
> We're *going for* a *car* ride.
> *Fasten* the *seat* belt.
>> Let's *go* to *church.*
> We're *going for* a *car* ride.
> *Bumpety—bumpety—bump.*
>> Let's *go* to *church.*
> We're *done* with our *ride.*
> We'll *sing* and *pray.*
>> Let's *go* to *church.*

> Dear Jesus,
>> Thank You for my church. Amen.

To the adult: *Going to church with a young child isn't always easy. But regular worship participation demonstrates to children the importance you place on going to church. And church-going is more than just a good tradition. Your child will grow up knowing that church is a happy place to learn about Jesus.*

Nothing can hide from [the sun's] heat.

Psalm 19:6

Hot Weather

Instructions: Act out this verse with your child.

It's so hot today,
An ice cream cone would melt.
Drip, drip, drip, right into my
    mouth.

It's so hot today,
A Popsicle would melt.
Drip, drip, drip, right into my
    mouth.

It's so hot today,
An ice cube would melt.
Drip, drip, drip, right into my
    mouth.

To the adult: *Children naturally want to be outside and in water on hot summer days. A bath, complete with bubbles, offers a welcome retreat from the sun. You might enjoy one too!*

Dear Jesus,
   Thanks for cold foods that melt
   on hot days. Amen.

Trust in the Lord, rely on your God.

Isaiah 50:10

Vacation

Instructions: Act out this verse and make the sounds in it with your child.

I'm on vacation in a car.
I sit, sit, sit.
Jesus comes along with me.
Honk! Honk! Honk!

I'm on vacation in a plane.
I fly, fly, fly.
Jesus comes along with me.
Zoom! Zoom! Zoom!

I'm on vacation in a train.
I go bumpety, bumpety, bump.
Jesus comes along with me.
Whoo! Whoo! Whoo!

I'm on vacation in a boat.
I splash, splash, splash.
Jesus comes along with me.
Varoom! Varoom! Varoom.!

To the adult: *Finding devotional time on vacation can be as challenging as finding devotional time at home. It's easiest to add a few minutes to a daily activity that you'd do wherever you are. A few minutes after supper, or before brushing teeth at night, or whenever you normally plan devotions also gives your child the security of a familiar routine.*

Dear Jesus,
   I'm glad You're always with me. Amen.

I am the One who created you.

Isaiah 44:24

Farm Animals

Instructions: Make the animal
sounds in this verse with your child.

A rooster crows cock-a-doodle-do.
A cow gives out a great big moo.
A chicken in a coop goes cluck.
You know at a quack, that it's a duck.
Who made animals quack, cluck,
    and moo?
God gave them voices. That's who!

To the adult: *Young children are often afraid the first time they
see live farm animals. To get an idea of just how large a horse or
cow appears to a young child, crouch in front of the animal. Then
you will be about the same height as a two- or three-year-old. No
wonder a horse looks so big—it is!*

LITTLE VISITS FOR TODDLERS

Dear Jesus,
    Thank You for animals. Amen.

He turns darkness into daylight.

Amos 5:8

Wake Up!

Instructions: Act out this verse with your child.

On mornings when I am asleep, all cozy tucked
in bed,
I try to stay there, sound asleep, not even lift my
head.
But light is showing from outside; I see it round
my door.
So even though it's early yet, I jump onto the
floor.
I stretch my arms, my legs, and toes; I shake my
fingers too.
God gave a brand-new day to me, and there is
much to do.
"Wake up, wake up," I call out loud. "God gave
us a new day."
"Get up, get up," I call about. "Get up and start
this day."

> Dear Jesus,
> Thank You for today. Amen.

To the adult: *Young children often wake up earlier than their parents hope they would. Also, young children often think, "If I'm up, everyone else should be too." As soon as your child can play safely and independently, plan some "morning only" toys. Get them out the night before. Talk to your child about using them in the morning. Be sure "morning only" toys are put away before breakfast.*

*Shout for joy, you heavens! Shout, deep places
of the earth!*   Isaiah 44:23

Under, On, Above

Instructions: You'll need a chair (and your support!) or
a bed for this activity, or a tunnel your child has built
and a flat of blocks to climb on.

(*Your child is underneath something.*)
God made things under the ground:
- worms that wiggle, • moles that tunnel,
- carrots that grow down.

(*Your child stands up.*)
God made things on the ground:
- trees that blow in the wind,
- dogs that wag their tails,
- sunflowers that grow so tall.

(*Your child stands on top of something.*)
God made things above the ground:
- stars that twinkle, • birds that fly,
- rain that falls.

(*Your child gets down.*)
God made many things. And God made me!
Dear Jesus,
    Thanks for making so many neat things. Amen.

To the adult: *A life preserver easily demonstrates the concepts of
"under, on, above" to a child. Your child might enjoy "rescuing"
toy animals or dolls with a paper preserver. Cut a "donut" from a
brown paper bag. For a child-size vest-type play preserver, cut
down the length of a large brown paper bag, cut a round hole in
the bottom and a round hole on each side.*

Look how the wild flowers grow.

right
Matthew 6:28

Flower Time

Instructions: Act out this verse with your child.

The summer flowers stand up high
To stretch their necks and reach the
    sky.
They close up tight when day is done.
They open only for the sun.

When God sends rain, their heads
    droop low
As if to say, "Oh, yes, we know.
"We need the rain. It feels so good.
"God cares for us. We knew He would."

God sends to flowers rain and sun.
He cares for each, yes, every one.
And we can feel this same way too:
God cares for me. He cares for you.

To the adult: *This is a great time for a mid-summer safety check. In spring, adults who live around young children are usually careful with weed trimmers, lawn equipment, and garden tools. By July, though, it's easy to get a little careless. Carefully reexamine outdoor areas used by your young child. Also check riding toys and swings for loose bolts or bolt covers that have come off.*

Dear Jesus,
 Thank You for taking care of me this
 summer. Amen.

God is the One who made the mountains.

Amos 4:13

Climbing a Mountain

Instructions: Act out this verse with your child.

I'm climbing up a mountain
To see what God has made.
I'm climbing up a mountain
Through sun and clouds and shade.

I'm climbing up a mountain.
My legs are getting sore.
I'm climbing up a mountain.
Oh! Now I can see more.

I'm finally on the mountain.
Look at what I see:
The trees! The sky! The rivers!
God's world for you and me.

To the adult: *Look for "pretend" mountains for your young one to climb: a mound of laundry, a pile of dirt, etc. Encourage your child to make her own mountain in the sandbox. Sticks can be trees; a piece of paper colored with blue crayon makes a lake.*

Dear Jesus,
 Thank You for this wonderful world.
 Amen.

May the peoples praise You, O God.

Psalm 67:5

Going to a Fair

Instructions: Act out this verse with your child.

Kiddie cars
The little cars can go so fast.
Zoom! Zoom! Zoom!
They speed up fast and faster still.
Varoom! Varoom! Varoom!

Ferris wheel
The wheel I watch is very big;
It goes up to the sky.
My neck gets tired watching it,
The ferris wheel so high.

Merry-go-round
Round and round and round I go
On the merry-go-round.
Round and round and round I go
And never touch the ground.

To the adult: *Going to a fair can be fun. For a young child, though, a fair can be downright scary. Balloons pop, rides are noisy, people can be dressed in costumes—all of these elements that can be enjoyable for older children can make young children fearful. Gently introduce your child to fairs—and be ready to leave early if necessary.*

Dear Jesus,
 Thank You for people who take
 me to fun places. Amen.

Sing a new song to Him.

Psalm 33:3

Sunday

Instructions: Act out this verse with your child as you sing it to the tune of "Here We Go round the Mulberry Bush."

> Sunday is a special day,
> Special day, special day.
> Sunday is a special day,
> When we can walk to church.
>
> Sunday is a special day,
> Special day, special day.
> Sunday is a special day,
> When we can hop to church.
>
> Sunday is a special day,
> Special day, special day.
> Sunday is a special day,
> When we can jump to church.
>
> Sunday is a special day,
> Special day, special day.
> Sunday is a special day,
> When we can skip to church.

To the adult: *Use this verse next Sunday while you're helping your child get ready for church. Substitute your own words in the last line, for example: "Sunday is a special day, when we get dressed for church." Or "Sunday is a special day; we comb your hair for church."*

Dear Jesus,
    I'm glad I get to go to church. Amen.

Give us day by day the food we need.

Luke 11:3

That Tastes Great!

Instructions: Ask your child to rub his tummy when he hears the name of a food he likes.

God gives me carrots.
God gives me ice cream.
God gives me oatmeal.
God gives me hamburgers.
God gives me cheese.
God gives me milk.
God gives me hot dogs.

To the adult: *It's not always easy to create nutritious foods that appeal to young children. Try these snacks: Cube cheese. Put a pretzel stick into each cube. Or buy plastic party toothpicks, and let your child spear his own pineapple chunks. Use the same type of toothpick for a mini-fruit kebab. A toothpick will hold two pieces of fruit; grapes, banana slices, and melon balls work well. Watch your child closely while he eats from the toothpick.*

Dear Jesus,
   Thanks for foods that taste good. Amen.

The sun will not hurt you during the day.

Psalm 121:6

Keepin' Cool

What can I do on a hot
   summer day?
I can take a nap.
I can get all wet.
I can stay in the shade.
I can drink lemonade.
I can suck on some ice.
Ah—that will be nice.

Dear Jesus,
   Thank You for things to help
   me keep cool. Amen.

To the adult: *When a young child is out in the sun, a sunbonnet, baseball cap, or visor can help reduce the sun's glare in the child's eyes. A headcovering is especially important when a child is near water because she can get a sunburned scalp fairly quickly. (Remember, infants and very young children might not have the natural sun protection of a full head of hair.)*

Children are a gift from the Lord.

Psalm 127:3

Between

Instructions: Act out this verse with your child.

> God put my elbows between my
> wrists and my shoulders.
> God put my waist between my
> shoulders and my hips.
> God put my longest fingers between
> my thumbs and my pinkies.
> God put my legs between my ankles
> and my knees.
> God put my face between my two
> ears.
> God put my smile where everybody
> can see it!

> Dear Jesus,
> I like me. I like You. Amen.

To the adult: *A full-length mirror is one of the most important pieces of furniture to a child. Children need to spend time looking at themselves, who they are, and how they appear. Young children grow fast and change quickly. They need to be able to keep up, visually, with their own growth.*

Give thanks to the Lord Almighty.

Jeremiah 33:11

Round and Round

Instructions: Ask your child to respond with "round and round" and make circles in the air after each line.

> Stroller wheels
> *Round and round.*
> Car wheels
> *Round and round.*
> Bike wheels
> *Round and round.*
> Wagon wheels
> *Round and round.*
> Bus wheels
> *Round and round.*
> Tractor wheels
> *Round and round.*
> They all turn
> *Round and round.*

To the adult: *Help your child notice different kinds of wheels during the next few days. Look for wheels everywhere—you'll probably discover some in rather surprising places.*

Dear Jesus,
    Thanks for things that go round
    and round. Amen.

[God] fashioned the earth and all that lives there.

Isaiah 42:5

Summer Sounds

Instructions: Make the sounds in this verse with your child.

> I look out the window.
> What do I see?
> God's summertime world
> Calling to me.
>
> I listen with care
> And hear many a sound.
> For summertime noises
> Are circling round.
>
> - A lawn mower roars.
> - A dog barks loudly.
> - Leaves rustle softly.
> - A bird chirps sweetly.
>
> I look out the window, and
>   what do I see?
> God's summertime world
>   calling to me.

To the adult: *Joining other children for play happens easily on summer days. But actual playing "with" others takes time and experience. Plant the seeds of sharing early: It takes two to see-saw; swinging is more fun when you swing next to someone else; etc. Be patient and positive.*

Dear Jesus,
    I like to hear the sounds of summer.
    Amen.

I am the One who made the earth.

Isaiah 45:12

Summer Quiet

Instructions: Act out this verse with your child.

> I stand at the window, and what do I
>   hear?
> God's summertime world whispers
>   so near.
> Listen carefully, or you won't hear a
>   sound.
> For summertime's quiet as it circles
>   around.
>
> • An ice cube melts.
> • A tadpole swims.
> • A bird finds a worm.
> • The grass grows.
>
> I stand at the window, and what do I
>   hear?
> God's summertime world whispers
>   so near.

To the adult: *Playing with salt is a quiet activity on a summer day. Empty a salt shaker into an old shoe box. Your child can trace shapes and letters with his finger. When play is over, your child can put on the lid and put away the box. Putting away even a simple toy like this is a great way to practice independent skills.*

Dear Jesus,
 Thank You for the softness of summer.
 Amen.

Sing, heavens! Shout for joy, earth!

Isaiah 49:13

The Park

Instructions: Act out this verse with your child.

The climber
Up the rungs I go
As I climb so high.
Step up, step up, step up, step up,
Way up to the sky.

The swing
The swing goes higher, higher still.
The wind blows right by me.
Now I swing so high I squeal.
Whee! Whee! Whee!

The seesaw
Up and down, up and down,
I must hold so tight.
Up so high, now down so low.
This ride is a delight.

Dear Jesus,
Thank You for fun places. Amen.

To the adult: *Time on a playground brings a child close to "heaven on earth." A playground visit can be brief, but it usually is a great experience. And the best might be yet to come: A young child usually sleeps very well after an outing at the park!*

Let us kneel before the Lord, our Maker!

Psalm 95:6

Up and Down

Instructions: Act out this verse with your child.

Here I go up. Here I go down.
What goes up?
- the barber's chair
- an elevator
- and me!

Here I go down. Here I go up.
What goes down?
- the barber's chair
- an elevator
- and me!

Here I go up. Here I go down.
Here I go up and down.
Now I'll kneel and pray.

Dear Jesus,
    Up and down I go each day. Thank
    You, Lord, I now will pray. Amen.

To the adult: *Up and down are some of the first directional words a young child understands. Right and left are two of the last directional words a child comprehends. In the meantime, use all kinds of directional words whenever possible. Giving specific directions will enrich your child's vocabulary and understanding.*

Sing to the Lord, all the world!

Psalm 100:1

A Joyful Noise

Instructions: Act out this verse and make the sounds in it with your child.

> The writer in the Bible says,
>   "Make a joyful noise."
> So listen as I shout hooray like
>   other girls and boys.
> Jesus is my Lord.
>   I can jump up high.
> Jesus is my Lord.
>   I can reach the sky.
> Jesus is my Lord.
>   I can wiggle my nose.
> Jesus is my Lord. I can tap my toes.
> Jesus is my Lord. I can turn around.
> Jesus is my Lord.
>   I can touch the ground.
> Praise the Lord!

To the adult: *Many parents pray that their child will grow up happy in the Lord. By using this book, you are taking the time and making the effort to help that happen. What a blessing you are to one of God's young children!*

Dear Jesus,
   Thank You for all the things I can do.
   Amen.

My children, our love … must be true love.

1 John 3:18

Listen to Me!

Instructions: Make the sounds described in this verse with your child.

I can make a sound like a car.
I can make a sound like a vacuum cleaner.
I can make a sound like a baby.
I can make a sound like a clock.
I can make a sound like a hammer.
I can sing a song to Jesus.
(*If your child hesitates, sing "Jesus Loves Me" with your child.*)
Jesus loves me, this I know, for the Bible tells me so.
Little ones to Him belong; they are weak, but He is strong.
Yes, Jesus loves me; yes, Jesus loves me. Yes, Jesus loves me; the Bible tells me so.

To the adult: *Help your child make music with water glasses. Fill glass drinking glasses with various amounts of water. Your child can lightly tap each glass with a spoon, then listen to the different pitches. Sing "Jesus Loves Me" again as your child taps the tune on the glasses. (As with any activity involving breakables, please carefully supervise your child.)*

Dear Jesus,
   I like to sing to You. Amen.

I have called you by name—you are mine.

Isaiah 43:1

A Rainbow Person

Instructions: Give your child a mirror to help him answer these questions.

What color eyes did God give you?
What color hair did God give you?
What color skin did God give you?
What color eyebrows did God give you?
(*Now encourage your child to
respond with the answers.*)

God gave me

_____ eyes.

God gave me

_____ hair.

God gave me

_____ skin.

God gave me

_____ eyebrows.
God made me a rainbow person.

To the adult: *Do this activity again and ask your child to describe colors God made you.*

Dear Jesus,
  Thank You for making me so
  color-full. Amen.

I create both light and darkness.

Isaiah 45:7

Day and Night

Instructions: Act out this verse with your child.

In the daytime, the sun shines.
In the daytime, the birds chirp.
In the daytime, squirrels hop from
   tree to tree.
I run and jump and play.
And Jesus is with me.

The night comes.
In the nighttime, the sun goes
   down.
In the nighttime, the birds sleep.
In the nighttime, the squirrels
   curl up.
I fall asleep in bed.
And Jesus is with me.

To the adult: *Fear of the dark is common among young children. Encourage your child to talk about being afraid. When appropriate, talk about times when you were afraid. Children need to understand it's okay to be scared, but help them find comfort in knowing that Jesus is always with them.*

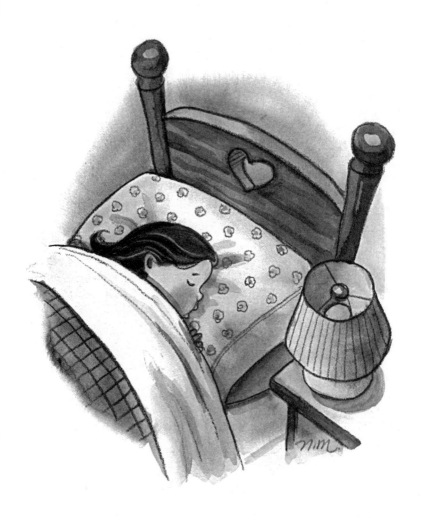

Dear Jesus,
   Thank You for always being with
   me. Amen.

Show me a man who does a good job.

Proverbs 22:29

Whoops!

Instructions: Act out this verse with your child.

When a button falls off—whoops!
We need to sew.
In and out, in and out—sew the button.
Thanks, God, for people who sew buttons.

When a nail comes loose—whoops!
We need to hammer.
Tap, tap, tap, tap—hammer the nail.
Thanks, God, for people who hammer nails.

When a tire goes flat—whoops!
We need to pump.
Whoosh-air, whoosh-air—pump the tire.
Thanks, God, for people who fix tires.

To the adult: *A child's circle of acquaintances gradually expands from family to friends to the neighborhood. Your child will first identify people by the uniforms they wear: nurse, letter carrier, store clerk, baseball player. A worn shirt can easily become a "uniform" for your child's playtime. For example: a white, adult-size shirt with rolled up sleeves makes a great "uniform" for any junior-size health worker.*

LITTLE VISITS FOR TODDLERS

Dear Jesus,
    Thanks for people who do all sorts
    of jobs. Amen.

I made you and will care for you.

Isaiah 46:4

Fingers

Instructions: Help your child use her fingers during this verse.

My fingers, I have 10 of them,
Do so very much.
They pull, they rub, they tap and
　flop,
And now they even touch.
They point to God's up-high blue
　sky
And to the ground below.
They snap, they bend, they wiggle,
And reach down to touch a toe.
My fingers can move back and forth
As trees sway in the breeze.
My fingers are so quiet
As I pray upon my knees.

Dear Jesus,
　Thanks for fingers that help me
　touch and hug. Amen.

To the adult: *How many other groups of 10 can your child count? Begin with her fingers, toes, your fingers, strands of hair, etc.*

*Do what your father tells you and never forget what
your mother taught you.*   Proverbs 6:20

Huggin' Time

Instructions: Hug your young child where indicated.

Here's a special hug; it's meant for only
you.
You're a favorite person; I love the things
we do.

Here's a special hug because I love you so,
Like Jesus loved His friends those many
years ago.

Here's a special hug because you are so
dear.
And even when I can't be close, I know that
God is near.

Here's a very special hug, because I'm filled
with love
For you, the other dear ones, and Jesus
from above.

Dear Jesus,
Thanks for somebody who loves me.
Amen.

To the adult: *As children grow up, we quite naturally spend less time
cuddling them. But even your two-year-old, who sometimes isn't too
lovable, needs hugs. Parents need hugs too. Read this devotion again;
this time your child can be the hugger, and you can be the huggee!*

The trees in the woods will shout for joy.

Psalm 96:12

Treehouses

Instructions: If possible, do this activity outdoors. Start a short distance from a tree. Your child can run back and forth to the tree as he acts out each verse. Indoors, substitute any piece of furniture for the "tree."

> "It's my house," says the bird.
>   Flap, flap, flap to the tree.
>   God made trees for birds.
>
> "It's my house," says the squir-
>   rel. Scamper, scamper, scam-
>   per to the tree. God made
>   trees for squirrels.
>
> "It's my house," says the ant.
>   Walk, walk, walk to the tree.
>   God made trees for ants.
>
> "It's my playhouse," says the
>   child. Run, run, run to the
>   tree. God made trees for me!

To the adult: *Fall housecleaning can uncover wonderful raw materials for children to use in sorting, dressing up, and creating works of art. Throw everything in a "not junk box." As long as there's nothing sharp or dangerous, your child will enjoy the "treasure box" on some long winter day.*

Dear Jesus,
    Thanks for trees. Amen.

It is good to be able to enjoy the pleasant light of day.

Ecclesiastes 11:7

Watch Me!

Instructions: Act out this verse with your child.

1.
Watch me.
I can twirl around one time.

1–2.
Watch me.
I can jump two times.

1–2–3.
Watch me.
I can hop on one foot three
    times.

1–2–3–4.
Watch me.
I can hop on the other foot
    four times.

1–2–3–4–5.
Watch me.
I can give you five kisses!

To the adult: *Did you and your child laugh together today? So much of parenting is hard work that it's tempting to forget to have fun. Take time out for fun—with activities like these—the next time you feel grumpy.*

Dear Jesus,
Thanks for Your fun times. Amen.

Go up on a high mountain and proclaim the good news!   Isaiah 40:9

Mountains and Plains

Instructions: You and your child can wave your hands up in the air for the "mountains" and down near the ground for the "plains."

God put trees
High in the mountains,
Down on the plains.

God put animals
High in the mountains,
Down on the plains.

God put birds
High in the mountains,
Down on the plains.

God put flowers
High in the mountains,
Down on the plains.

God put me right here!

To the adult: *Read this verse slowly the first time, then speed up the pace each time you repeat it. This activity easily bridges the gap between older and younger children, especially as the pace increases.*

Dear Jesus,
    I'm glad You put me here. Amen.

Then He got up and ordered the winds and the waves to stop, and there was a great calm.   Matthew 8:26

The Storm

Instructions: Give your child two pan lids to bang together where indicated.

In a small boat,
On a big lake,
Went Jesus and His friends.

A storm came up (*bang, bang*),
The sky grew dark (*bang, bang*),
Over Jesus and His friends.

The lightning cracked (*bang, bang*),
The thunder crashed (*bang, bang*),
Around Jesus and His friends.

"Wake up, wake up" (*bang, bang*),
The people said (*bang, bang*).
"Wake, Jesus!" called His friends.

Jesus woke up and said, "Be still."
The storm was done
For Jesus and His friends.

Dear Jesus,
Storms can be scary. I'm glad You
helped Your friends. Amen.

To the adult: *Your child can reenact this story in the bathroom sink. Shape aluminum foil into a "boat." (For a fancy mast, stick a toothpick into play dough or into a prune.) Read the story again without the "bang, bang."*

O Lord, my God, how great You are!

Psalm 104:1

Climb Up

Instructions: Act out this verse with your child by walking your fingers up your arms. At the end, your fingers should be near your faces.

> A hill.
> A hill of sand.
> A hill of sand on the sidewalk.
>
> Climb up.
> Climb up to the top.
> Climb up to the top of the anthill.
>
> God watches.
> God watches over His creatures.
> God watches over His creatures and me.

> Dear Jesus,
> I know You watch over little things
> like ants.
> I'm glad You watch over big people like me.
> Amen.

To the adult: *Ants are child-size creatures that build child-size places to live. Your child will enjoy playing with a stick and a crawling ant. Show her how to be gentle with God's creatures.*

I will sing You a new song, O God.

Psalm 144:9

Singing Fun

Instructions: Act out this verse with your child as you sing it to the tune of "Twinkle, Twinkle, Little Star."

I can clap my hands up high.
Watch me clap them in the sky.
Take my hands and clap, clap, clap.
Now my feet go tap, tap, tap.
I am Jesus' child I know,
For the Bible tells me so.

I can walk on my tiptoes.
Then reach up and touch my nose.
Take my fingers tap, tap, tap.
Make my feet go stamp, stamp, stamp.
I am Jesus' little one.
Jesus loves me, God's dear Son.

God gives me so many parts:
Hands and shoulders, feet and heart.
For it's with my heart I love
Jesus, Son of God, above.
He alone created me,
And He guides me happily.

To the adult: *Learning about his body—and what it can do—is a major part of life for your young child. He's probably learning about snaps and buttons and zippers too. Tying a shoelace, though, is a complicated activity that he'll learn much later. Always encourage, never push.*

Dear Jesus,
 I like to sing about You. Amen.

Give thanks to the Lord, proclaim His greatness.
Psalm 105:1

Sit a Spell

Instructions: Pull a chair—preferably child-size—into the center of the room for your child to sit on during this devotion. Act out this verse with your child.

> I can sit on a bike and pedal
>   fast.
> I can sit in the car, "Please step
>   on the gas."
> I can sit on a park bench and
>   watch kites fly.
>
> I can sit in an airplane; see
>   houses go by.
> I can sit in a church to pray
>   and sing.
> That's where I thank God for
>   everything.

To the adult: *Your child can easily set up the seats for an "airplane" or "car." Line up chairs in pairs. Cut a 2"-wide strip from a paper bag that's long enough to go across the chair. Lay it on each chair for a seat belt.*

Dear Jesus,
   Thanks for places to go and things to
   see. Amen.

The land has produced its harvest.

Psalm 67:6

It All Falls Down

Instructions: Act out this verse with your child.

The leaves fall: swish, swish.
The acorns fall: kerplop,
   kerplop.
The raindrops fall: drip, drip.
The pinecones fall: plop, plop.

Many things fall in autumn.
Soon God will send something
   else to fall.
The snow will fall: softly, softly.
Have a good winter's nap,
   earth.

To the adult: *Now is the time to plan for that first really cold day. Your young child has probably grown a lot since last year. Keep one warm outfit handy for your child so outside play is possible, even if temperatures drop suddenly.*

Dear Jesus,
My favorite thing about autumn
is _____ . Amen.

As I lie in bed, I remember You.

Psalm 63:6

Good Night

Instructions: Use this verse with your child at bedtime.

When the sky is dark and the sun goes
down,
It's nighttime. It's not light-time.
Good night, sun.

When the sky is dark and the moon
comes up,
It's nighttime. It's not light-time.
Good night, moon.

When the sky is dark and the stars
come out,
It's nighttime. It's not light-time.
Good night, stars.

When the sky is dark,
The sun goes down,
The moon comes up,
The stars come out.
It's nighttime. It's not light-time.
It's my bedtime.
Good night, God.

To the adult: *As a child, did you have a favorite bedtime song or lullaby? Ask family members and relatives to help you tape "family favorite" lullabies. Then even your very young child can fall asleep listening to familiar voices continuing a family tradition.*

Dear Jesus,
 Thank You for the stars so bright and the moon
 That lightens up the night. Amen.

The Lord will guard you; He is by your side
to protect you.   Psalm 121:5

My Friend, Jesus

Instructions: Act out this verse with your child.

I can walk all alone.
I can walk with a friend.
Jesus walks with me.

I can walk very fast.
I can walk very slow.
Jesus walks with me.

I can walk with tiny steps.
I can walk with giant steps.
Jesus walks with me.

To the adult: *How does your child view Jesus? Young children often develop "imaginary friends." Some young children even see Jesus in this way. Developmentally, we know this is appropriate. Sharing the Christian faith with a child is a wonderful experience because soon, the child will understand that Jesus is real and offers so much more than an imaginary friend.*

Dear Jesus,
    Thanks for being with me. Amen.

*Whoever believes that Jesus is the Messiah
is a child of God.* 1 John 5:1

I Can

Instructions: Ask your child to nod yes to everything she can do.

> I can sneeze.
> I can crawl.
> I can stamp my feet.
> I can whisper.
> I can cough.
> I can shake hands.
> I can say a prayer to Jesus.

> Dear Jesus,
> Thank You for helping me
> grow up. Amen.

To the adult: *It's important to emphasize the "can dos" when working with young children. Being positive, beginning activities with a smile, and saying, "You did a good job," are very important in positive parenting. You are, right now, doing one of the most important actions any parent can do: helping a young child grow with Jesus. That's a "can do" that lasts a lifetime and beyond.*

I was glad when they said to me,
"Let us go to the Lord's house."   *Psalm 122:1*

Building Blocks

Instructions: Help your child count 1–2–3.

Let's build a church now:
1–2–3.
Let's build it high
For you and me.
Let's walk inside now:
1–2–3.
Let's pray to Jesus
Just you and me.

Dear Jesus,
I like to go to church. Amen.

To the adult: *Does your child build "houses" that don't look like houses? Or does your toddler "play blocks" by simply carrying around a block? There are distinct developmental stages to block building. Your child will progress from simply holding a block to creating complicated structures that represent something in "real life." Children go through the same stages but spend varying amounts of time at each stage.*

What a rich harvest Your goodness provides!

Psalm 65:11

What's Cooking?

Instructions: You and your child can clap once on each syllable of this verse.

This good food tastes airy.
This good food has bumps.
This good food sounds crunchy.
This good food looks white.
This good food even smells good.
This good food is popcorn!

To the adult: *You and your child can have fun "popping" popcorn. Take an old crib or twin sheet. You and your child hold opposite sides of the sheet. Then raise and lower the sheet while you "pop" corn. White ping pong balls make ideal "corn" to bounce up and down, but a child's shoe also works well. This is great fun when you need a break from routine.*

Dear Jesus,
    Thanks for fun food like popcorn. Amen.

The hillsides are full of joy.

Psalm 65:12

Autumn Song

Instructions: Act out this verse with your child as you sing it to the tune of "Frère Jacques" ("Are You Sleeping").

Leaves are falling,
Leaves are falling,
All around, all around.
Red and yellow twirling.
God sends winds to swirl them
To the ground,
To the ground.

Pinecones falling,
Pinecones falling,
All around, all around.
Cracking as they tumble.
Breaking as they crumble
On the ground,
On the ground.

To the adult: *With your help, your child can make a leaf rubbing. Peel a crayon. Lay a thin piece of paper over a leaf your child has found. Help your child rub the crayon on the paper that covers the leaf.*

Dear Jesus,
  I know fall is when the earth gets
  ready to take a nap. Amen.

Don't let anything worry you.

Ecclesiastes 11:10

Scary Times

Instructions: You and your child can clap hands at every word-sound (in italics).

When a balloon goes *pop*,
Sometimes I get scared.

When thunder goes *clap*,
Sometimes I get scared.

When something falls with a
    boom,
Sometimes I get scared.

When a clown says *boo*,
Sometimes I get scared.

When a firecracker goes *bang*,
Sometimes I get scared.

That's when I pray.

To the adult: *Some of your young child's fears are easy to under-stand: fear of the dark, storms, big dogs. But other fears might seem irrational: the fear of balloons, for example, or candles on a birthday cake. Some children go to extraordinary lengths (such as hiding under a table at a birthday party!) to get away from such things. During these times, provide support and quiet assurance, and know that the fear will probably dissolve within the next year or so.*

LITTLE VISITS FOR TODDLERS

Dear Jesus,
    Be with me. Amen.

God has blessed us.

Psalm 67:7

Cornstalks

Instructions: Act out this verse with your child.

Five cornstalks standing
straight and tall.
Five cornstalks standing;
soon they'll fall.
The farmer will cut them
down.
1–2–3–4–5 touch the
ground.
This harvest time brings
special cheer.
Pop, pop, pop is what I
hear!

Dear Jesus,
Thanks for popcorn. Amen.

To the adult: *Warnings from the medical community encourage adults to carefully supervise children under three when they eat foods such as popcorn and peanuts.*

How good it is to give thanks to You, O Lord.

Psalm 92:1

Brown Signs

Instructions: Look outside for this activity.

There are many signs of fall. See
if you can guess these riddles.
It is brown. It fell from a tree. I
rake it up.
It is a _____ (*leaf*).
It is brown. It scampers around. It
looks for nuts to bury. It has a
bushy tail.
It is a _____ (*squirrel*).
It is brown now. It was green in
summer. It grew so long that
we cut it with a lawn mower.
It is _____ (*grass*).

Dear Jesus,
It's autumn. You're with me.
Thanks. Amen.

To the adult: *Your child might want to carry a sand pail along on
your next walk. Help him collect things from nature that are brown.*

Worship the Lord with joy.

Psalm 100:2

Sounds for Jesus

Instructions: Make the sounds in this verse with your child.

A little train said, "Toot, toot."
I can "toot" for Jesus.
Toot-toot-toot. Praise God!

A little cement mixer said, "Rumble, rumble."
I can "rumble" for Jesus.
Rumble-rumble-rumble. Praise God!

A little fire engine said, "Whirr, whirr."
I can "whirr" for Jesus.
Whirr-whirr-whirr. Praise God!

A little boat said, "Putt, putt."
I can "putt" for Jesus.
Putt-putt-putt. Praise God!

A little child said, "I can make all those noises.
"I can toot-toot.
"I can rumble-rumble.
"I can whirr-whirr.
"I can putt-putt.
"I can praise God.
"I can also tell Jesus I love Him."

To the adult: *How many sounds can your child make using an empty toilet-paper roll?*

Dear Jesus,
   I love You. Amen.

Let the children come to Me and do not stop them.

Matthew 19:14

"Come to Me"

Instructions: Help your child count on her fingers.

Once Jesus called some little ones,
"Come here and sit near me.
"I want to see each one of you,
"So come now, 1–2–3."

The children came to Jesus fast;
They sat upon His knee.
1–2–3–4–5–6–7–8
"I'm glad you came to me."

Now Jesus calls us—you and me—
Today and every day.
1–2–3–4–5–6–7–8
He'd like to hear us pray.

To the adult: *Help your child act out this Bible story with stuffed animals and toys.*

Dear Jesus,
   I'm glad I'm important to You. Amen.

God looked at everything He had made,
and He was very pleased.   Genesis 1:31

Leaf Turnover

Instructions: Do this activity outside with
your child or bring a few leaves indoors.

Turn over a leaf.
What do I see?
Highways for plant food
and water.

Turn over a leaf.
What do I see?
Some colors of God's
rainbow.

Turn over a leaf.
What do I see?
Some humps and bumps
that I can feel.

To the adult: *Make it easy for your young child to learn independence doing autumn clean-up chores. A child can handle a small-size rake, but he will also need a place to store the rake. Children can put away sandbox toys for the winter, but storage must be low to the ground. Build in ways, right now, that help your young child be independent.*

Dear Jesus,
    Thank You for autumn. Amen.

Come and see what the Lord has done.

Psalm 46:8

Animals in Autumn

Instructions: Act out this verse with your child.

> The squirrels scamper here and
>   there with nuts to bury deep.
> They'll gobble up those nuts
>   for snacks when they wake up
>   from sleep.
> The snakes squirm in the
>   forest with their tummies
>   on the ground.
> They slither to a hiding place so
>   they will not be found.
> The birds fly south across the sky,
>   wings flapping as they go.
> They are in such a hurry now not
>   even one is slow.
> Why do God's woodland creatures
>   all now slither, scamper, fly?
> They know the winter's coming;
>   so to fall they say, "Good-bye."

To the adult: *On the next walk with your child, talk about how God's world is protected during the winter. Bark is a "coat" for a tree. Leaves provide a "blanket" for the ground. Animals, even the family dog, might grow a thicker coat, etc.*

Dear Jesus,
 Thank You for telling the animals
 how to get ready for winter. Amen.

It is love, then, that you should strive for.

1 Corinthians 14:1

Tap a Tune

Instructions: Help your child tap a spoon on the table on every word of this echo verse. You say a line; your child will repeat it while tapping.

I love Jesus.
I love Jesus.
You love Jesus.
You love Jesus.
We love Jesus.
We love Jesus.
I tell others.
I tell others.
You tell others.
You tell others.
We tell others.
We tell others.
I'm His helper.
I'm His helper.
You're His helper.
You're His helper.
We're His helpers.
We're His helpers.

To the adult: *When it comes to rhythm, children are natural music makers. They will have fun clapping the rhythm of the names of those who love them: Jesus, Mommy, Grandpa, sister, etc.*

Dear Jesus,
  I like telling people about You.
  Amen.

Praise Him for the mighty things He has done.

Psalm 150:2

Ten

Instructions: Help your child count.

I remember when it was winter.
I counted all my fingers in my gloves.
1–2–3–4–5–6–7–8–9–10

I remember when it was spring.
I counted 10 raindrops in the puddle.
1–2–3–4–5–6–7–8–9–10

I remember when it was summer.
I counted my toes wiggling in the pool.
1–2–3–4–5–6–7–8–9–10

Now it is autumn.
I can count 10 leaves on the ground.
1–2–3–4–5–6–7–8–9–10

Dear Jesus,
    Thanks for all the times of year. Amen.

To the adult: *Some events in our lives as parents will be etched forever in our memories. But much of our time simply floats by. Photographs can help us "remember when." Consider taking a picture of your child next to a small tree or shrub on the first day of each new season. Date your photo. Some parents like to take this idea a bit further and plant a tree on a child's birthday and then use that child's tree in the photos. "Me and my tree" becomes a great memory book for the child and parent.*

The Lord takes pleasure in His people.

Psalm 149:4

Listen!

Instructions: Make the sounds
in this verse with your child.

God gave me ears so I can hear:
- a motorcycle roar—rrrrrr
- an ambulance siren—
  whooooooo
- a church bell—ding dong
- a train whistle—choo! choo!
"Happy Thanksgiving!"

Dear Jesus,
    Help me remember to say thank
    You for all You give. Amen.

To the adult: *Many parents keep baby books and picture records,
but a sound recording of your child's development can bring back
some of the happiest memories. As you talk with your baby and
listen to your toddler, turn on a tape to record those sounds. Just
capture the sounds and note the date; there will be time in the
future to "edit."*

I am the God who forgives your sins.

Isaiah 43:25

Let's Build

Instructions: Get a stack of building blocks or anything small that can be piled high for a tower: spools of thread, plastic containers, books, etc. Help your child count as you add to your steeple.

> Let's build a steeple, 1–2–3.
> Let's build a steeple,
>   just you and me.
> Let's build a steeple, 4–5–6.
>
> Let's build a steeple
>   made of bricks.
> Let's build a steeple, 7–8–9.
> Let's build a steeple.
>   Will it be fine?
> (*It falls.*) The steeple fell down.

To the adult: *We practice forgiveness each day. As adults, we need to give children the assurance of our forgiveness and Christ's forgiveness. But we also need to remember that when we're not the parent we want to be or hope to be God forgives us too. He gives us the chance to try again.*

Dear Jesus,
   Sometimes it happens: things
   don't work right.
   But Jesus forgives me and says,
   "It's all right." Amen.

When He spoke, the world was created.

Psalm 33:9

A Pet

Instructions: Act out this verse with your child.

A pet might swim in a bowl.
A pet might dig a big hole.
A pet might sit in your lap.
A pet would be good for that!

A pet might chirp tweet, tweet, tweet.
A pet might kiss you, oh, so sweet.
A pet might woof bow, wow, wow.
A pet might whisper meow.

To the adult: *Children and pets go together. That's often true in artists' illustrations but only sometimes true in life. For a young child, the best pet might live at Grandma's or a neighbor's.*

Dear Jesus,
    Thank You for creating pets. Amen.

Your praise ... is sung by children.

Psalm 8:1–2

Fall Is Here

Instructions: Act out this verse with your child as you sing it to the tune of "Here We Go round the Mulberry Bush."

Watch me as I rake the leaves,
Rake the leaves, rake the leaves.
Watch me as I rake the leaves,
God says fall is here.

Watch me as I bake a pie,
Bake a pie, bake a pie.
Watch me as I bake a pie,
From a big, fat pumpkin.

Watch me as I put away,
Put away, put away.
Watch me as I put away,
All my summer toys.

To the adult: *Help your child make up her own verses for the song. For example: Put away summer clothes, take a nice long nap, etc.*

Dear Jesus,
Autumn is here, and I feel
_____ . Amen.

He supplies the needs of those who honor Him.

Psalm 145:19

Kitchen Fun

Instructions: Act out this verse with your child.

Sifting, sifting. We'll bake a pie.
Whoops! Don't touch.
The pan is hot.
Thank You, God, for food.

Stirring, stirring. Let's make some gravy.
Whoops! Don't touch.
The pot is hot.
Thank You, God, for food.

Kneading, kneading. We'll bake some bread.
Whoops! Don't touch.
The bread will rise.
Thank You, God, for food.

Sniffing, sniffing. My nose is working.
Great! Let's eat.
God gives us food.
Thank You, God, for food.

Dear Jesus,
My favorite Thanksgiving Day food is
_____ . Amen.

To the adult: *Even a young child can help make finger gelatin. Pour four small packages of any flavor gelatin into 2 ½ cups boiling water in a bowl. Stir to dissolve. Pour the gelatin into 8" or 9" square pan. Chill at least four hours. Cut into holiday shapes with cookie cutters. The scraps taste great too!*

Come and see what God has done.

Psalm 66:5

Finger Fun

Instructions: Act out this verse with your child.

These are my ten fingers;
God gave them all to me.
These are my two thumbs;
I wiggle them now, see?
My little pinkies are so small
That I just let them be.
And then that leaves the other
ones; I count them 1, 2, 3.
These are my ten fingers;
God gave them all to me.

Dear Jesus,
I pray when my fingers go
together. Thank You, Jesus.
Amen.

To the adult: *Young children delight in seeing how their fingers can help make a "hand turkey." Spread out your child's hand on a piece of paper. Trace around each of the fingers up to the wrist. A turkey will appear!*

I will give You thanks forever.

Psalm 30:12

The Garage

Instructions: Help your child learn how the various tools are used.

What's in a garage?

A rake gathers the leaves.
Leaves fall from the trees.
Rake-rake-rake.

A shovel moves the snow
When the cold winds blow.
Shovel-shovel-shovel.

A hoe digs the ground
When weeds are around.
Dig-dig-dig.

A car? Oh, yes.
A car has a place in the leftover space!
Varoom-varoom.

To the adult: *How do you store all those bulky child-related "essentials"? A "parking lot" will help your young child develop good habits of putting away. In the garage, for example, use chalk or masking tape to mark places on the floor for the stroller and tricycle. You and your child can find pictures of similar items in a catalog, cut out the pictures, and paste them on paper. Hang the paper on the wall in the appropriate "parking space." Your child will find it great fun to be "parking lot supervisor."*

230   LITTLE VISITS FOR TODDLERS

Dear Jesus,
   Thanks for things and places to keep them
   Amen.

[God] changes rocks into pools of water.

Psalm 114:8

Water

Instructions: Help your child
show the ways he uses water.

I can wash my face.
Splash, splash, splash.
I can water the flowers.
Drink, drink, drink.
I can clean my toys.
Scrub, scrub, scrub.
I can hold an umbrella.
Drip, drip, drop.

Dear Jesus,
Water feels wet. I like water when
_____ . Amen.

To the adult: *Collect a group of bathtub toys that float: Styrofoam cups, bits of aluminum foil, plastic silverware. Your child might enjoy a "pretend" floating meal on a thin plastic place mat!*

Let's go to Bethlehem.

Luke 2:15

What Happened?

Instructions: Make the sounds in this verse with your child.

When Jesus was born, a cow might
   have mooed.
When Jesus was born, a dove
   might have cooed.
When Jesus was born, a donkey
   might have brayed.
When Jesus was born, a horse
   might have neighed.
Now Jesus was born, and I can say,
"Jesus of Bethl'em, Happy
   Birthday."

Dear Jesus,
   Christmas is coming. I'm glad. Amen.

To the adult: *Your child can make napkin rings to use for holiday meals. Cut off a 1″ strip from an empty toilet-paper roll. Then ask your child to decorate it with Christmas stickers.*

The water ... was a symbol pointing to baptism.

1 Peter 3:20–21

Tickle My Back!

Instructions: Ask your child to sit with her back facing you. Using your fingers, trace different Christmas symbols on your child's back. Can she guess what you're drawing? Use the extra clues if your child needs help.

Heart (*reminds us Jesus loves us*)
Candle (*something we put on Jesus' birthday cake*)

Star (*what the Wise Men looked at in the sky*)
Cross (*Jesus died for us*)

To the adult: *As the busy days of December tick away, use this game again with variations. Trace the first letter of your child's name, Jesus' name, etc. Playing "tickle my back" will give you and your child quality moments during this busy season—and a great excuse to sit down and rest!*

Dear Jesus,
    I liked this tickly game. Thanks for fun
    times like Your birthday. Amen.

Glory to God in the highest heaven.

Luke 2:14

C-H-R-I-S-T-M-A-S-Y

Instructions: Help your child use his fingers.

C is for Christmas, Jesus' birthday.

H is for happy, and that's for me.

R is for the robe that kept Jesus warm.

I is for innkeeper who lent a room free.

S is for star, high in the sky.

T is for three, the number of gifts He received.

M is for Mary, mother of the Babe.

A is for angels who looked so bright.

S is for shepherds who came right away.

Y is for you! Happy Jesus' birthday.

To the adult: *Even young children are introduced to the Santa versus Jesus struggle. When a child focuses on simple fingerplays such as this, and enjoys a happy celebration of Jesus' birth, no one even thinks of Santa!*

Dear Jesus,
I used my fingers, all of them, to tell
Your birthday story again. Amen.

Jesus was born in the town of Bethlehem.

Matthew 2:1

Christmas Fun

Instructions: Act out this verse with your child.

I would laugh
if the shepherd's staff
were a candy cane.
I would bite
a star cookie in the night,
but the Magi's star was real.
I like to eat
all kinds of Christmas treats
that remind me of Jesus.
But all the while,
as I smile, I'm most happy that
Jesus was born for me.

Dear Jesus,
Thank You for the fun times
of Christmas. Amen.

To the adult: *With the pressures of holiday activities, it's easy to lose sight of the true joy of Christmas. That's one thing that makes Christmas with a young child such fun: she laughs, smiles, and really enjoys. What a privilege to share a first, or second, or third Christmas with a child. As you experience the real joy of Christ's birth, may you have a most blessed Christmastide.*

I am here with good news for you.

Luke 2:10

Counting Up Christmas

Instructions: Act out this verse with your child. Begin with the little finger.

Here's the mother of Jesus (*little finger*), and Joseph stands so tall (*ring finger*).

Now two shepherds from the field. Do we have them all?

We're missing Baby Jesus (*thumb*), born on Christmas Day.

Happy birthday, Jesus, is what we have to say.

Dear Jesus,
Happy birthday. Amen.

To the adult: *This finger play is an easy way for a child to focus on the real meaning of Christmas. Your child might want to learn this and share it with friends and relatives during the holidays.*

They told them what the angel had said about the child.
Luke 2:17

Bake a Birthday Cake

Instructions: Act out this verse with your child as you sing it to the tune of "Here We Go round the Mulberry Bush."

This is the way I mix a cake,
mix a cake, mix a cake.
This is the way I mix a cake,
a birthday cake for Jesus.

This is the way I cut a cake,
cut a cake, cut a cake.
This is the way I cut a cake,
a birthday cake for Jesus.

This is the way I eat a cake,
eat a cake, eat a cake.
This is the way I eat a cake,
a birthday cake for Jesus.

To the adult: *Children can easily identify with the idea of Jesus' birthday. Some families serve a Jesus birthday cake for the holiday dessert. Your young child will love putting on candles and even arranging a small créche set on the frosted cake.*

Dear Jesus,
I love You. Amen.

This very day in David's town your Savior was born—Christ the Lord!

Luke 2:11

Ring, Ring

Instructions: Tie jingle bells onto your child's shoelaces or give her a bell to ring. A Christmas ornament bell works well.

> I can sing. I can sing.
>   Jesus is born.
>
> I can shout. I stamp
>   about. Jesus is born.
>
> I can clap. I can tap.
>   Jesus is born.
>
> I can tell, ring my bell.
>   Jesus is born.

To the adult: *Make a tape recording as you and your child sing Christmas carols. Try to tape your child's "telling" of the Christmas story, if appropriate. Date your tape. After the holidays, pack it away with the crèche set. Next year, start recording as your child helps you unpack the manger figures. The informal chatter of your own Christmas child will be a keepsake.*

Dear Jesus,
  My song today is "It's Your Birthday."
  Amen.

Let us walk in the light which the Lord gives us!

Isaiah 2:5

Blink, Blink

Instructions: Give your child a flashlight and tell him to turn it on every time you read, "Jesus, the Light of the world."

It's Christmas.
Jesus is born for me.
Jesus the Light of the world.

It's Christmas.
Jesus was born in Bethlehem.
Jesus the Light of the world.

It's Christmas.
Jesus is my Savior.
Jesus the Light of the world.

It's Christmas.
Happy birthday, Jesus.
Jesus the Light of the world.

To the adult: *A flashlight and batteries is a wonderful Christmas gift for a child. Take a flashlight along to the Christmas candlelight service, if you want. For a young child, the artificial light makes a good substitute for a candle dripping hot wax.*

LITTLE VISITS FOR TODDLERS

Dear Jesus,
   Happy Birthday. Amen.

The time came for her to have her baby.

Luke 2:6

What I Need for Christmas

Instructions: Act out this verse with your child.

What do I need for Christmas?
I need a tall, tall tree.
It must reach higher than I can,
Much higher up than me.

What do I need for Christmas?
I need a bell to ring.
"Ding dong, ding dong, ding"
Is what my bell will sing.

What do I need for Christmas?
I need a birthday time.
Jesus' happy birthday
Will make my Christmas fine.

Dear Jesus,
    Thank You for being born. Amen.

To the adult: *Some families put Christ in the center of their Christmas by adding one figure to the créche set each day. Mary, Joseph, and animals are set out, one each day, on the days before Christmas. Jesus is added on Christmas Day, and the shepherds, animals, and Magi after Christmas.*

You will find a baby wrapped in cloths.

Luke 2:12

Wrap It Up

Instructions: Act out this verse with your child.

When I wrap a Christmas present,
I cut some pretty paper.
I cover the box.
I tape the paper.
I tie a bow.
It's all done.

When God sent His present to us,
Mary wrapped God's Gift with care.
She folded the cloth round and round
And laid the Baby gently in a manger.
God sent the first Christmas present to us:
    Baby Jesus.

Dear Jesus,
    I'm glad You were born. Amen.

To the adult: *Large packages will be the easiest for your young child to wrap. Little gifts require too much fine motor control for most young children. If you involve your child in wrapping gifts— and that's a great idea—begin with an even surface, plan to hold the tape, and bring plenty of patience.*

[The star] went ahead of them.

Matthew 2:9–10

A Camel Ride

Instructions: Cut out a crown from a brown paper bag for your child to wear. It's also ideal if your child can ride "camel back" while the two of you act out this verse.

Please hop on a camel and go find Jesus.
Just watch for a big star and you'll find Jesus.
Ride, ride, the camel now to search for Jesus.
Stop! Ask people you meet,
   "Have you seen Jesus?"
Ride, ride the camel now to search for Jesus.
Follow the shining star. We're getting closer.
It stopped! The star stopped here.
   Where is the baby?
Get off the camel now. Where is the baby?
There's the star, over there.
   Where is the baby?
(*Walk toward your own créche.*)
Here is baby Jesus. We have found Jesus.

To the adult: *Your child can decorate her crown by gluing on scraps of wrapping paper.*

Dear Jesus,
I'm glad You were born. Amen.

I remember the days gone by; I think about all that You have done. Psalm 143:5

Good-Bye and Hello

Instructions: Act out this verse with your child.

I can wave good-bye.
I can give a good-bye hug.
I can smile good-bye.
I can give a good-bye kiss.
Good-bye, old year.

I can wave hello.
I can give a hello hug.
I can smile hello.
I can give a hello kiss.
Hello, new year.

To the adult: *You might be one of the few people at your home celebrating the gift of a new year. This is because a young child's new year begins and ends on his birthday. So—have a blessed new year!*

Dear Jesus,
    I end the old year with You. I will start
    the new year with You. Amen.

Topical Index

Scripture Index

Genesis

1:24	29, 18
1:25	42
1:31	214
2:7	112
7:8–9	40
8:22	49, 100

Psalm

3:5	34, 48
8:1–2	226
8:9	134
19:6	142
30:12	230
33:3	156
33:9	224
34:1	30
36:8	50
46:1	78
46:8	216
63:6	196
65:9	132
65:10	72, 104
65:11	202
65:12	138, 204
66:5	229
67:5	154
67:6	194
67:7	208
92:1	209
95:1	116, 141
95:6	98, 169
96:11	124
96:12	120, 182
100:1	170
100:2	210
103:5	128
104:1	189
104:24	61, 102
104:28	104
105:1	192
114:8	232
121:5	198
121:6	160
122:1	201
127:3	161
135:3	22
136:1	46
136:25	16
139:13	26, 80
143:5	252
144:9	190
145:15	68
145:19	228
147:16	18, 32
147:18	56
148:9–10	96
149:2	81
149:3	140
149:4	221
150:2	220
150:4	82

Proverbs

2:1	76
3:19	101
6:20	181
15:1	136
22:6	94
22:29	178

Ecclesiastes

3:1	86
3:6	24
3:11	129
11:7	184
11:9	121
11:10	206
12:1	84

Song of Songs

2:3	36
2:11	108